CLASSROOM TEACHER'S
ESL SURVIVAL KIT# 2

Elizabeth Claire • Judie Haynes

Illustrated by
J.D. Frazier and Don Martinetti

Edited by
John Chapman
Samantha Coles

Classroom Teacher's ESL Survival Kit # 2 by Elizabeth Claire and Judie Haynes

Original Publisher: Prentice Hall Regents, ISBN 0-13-299876-9

Acquisition Editor: Nancy Baxer
Electronic Production/Design Manager: Dominick Mosco
Creative Director: Paula Maylahn
Editorial/Production Supervision: Steve Jorgensen
Developmental Consultant: John Chapman
Page Composition: Steve Jorgensen
Cover Design: Wanda España
Production Coordinator: Ray Keating
Production Assistant: Kelly Tavares

This edition published by Eardley Publications
Saddle Brook, NJ 07663

Revision Coordinator: Samantha Coles
Cover Photo: Simon Krzic/Bigstockphoto.com

Printed in the United States of America

ISBN 987-0937630-41-9

Table of Contents

This book is dedicated to the courageous families who pack up their children and their belongings to take an enormous step across national borders to seek a better life, and to the memory of our own, ever-so-great, grandparents, who did the same.

Acknowledgments

This book was not written by the authors alone; it owes its existence to the contributions of many, many people. We are immensely grateful for their assistance, and would like to express our thanks

First, thanks to the teachers who asked for this book, to the teachers who provided feedback, and to the teachers who served as role models, demonstrating their caring and their effective interactions with newcomers. Special thanks to Marie Anello, Hazel Buchwald, Mary Jane Carroll, Nancy Chiang, Nancy DuBois, Arlene Dukette, Mimi Kim, Ann Urgo, and Ruth Weinstein.

Thanks to the countless students who showed us where the bumpy places were.

Thanks (again) to Nancy Baxer for all-round inspiration, caring, vision, encouragement, management, foresight, trouble-shooting, hand-holding, and friendship.

Thanks to John Chapman for his watchful eye on content, design, wording, teacher's directions, and appropriateness of the activities.

Thanks to Joe Frazier for his historic scenes and delightful characters, and to Don Martinelli for his professional execution of a zillion animals, maps and assorted shapes and objects.

Thanks to Janet Johnston for an extraordinary copyediting job.

Thanks to Dominick Mosco for his calm and competence in overseeing production and to Steve Jorgensen for gracefully handling the exacting minutiae of line-by-line accuracy and fit, home deliveries of the manuscript and the utmost patience in getting all the pices to fit together.

Thanks to Stu Tuchfeld for outstanding results in bringing Kit #1 to classroom teachers in New York City, thereby creating the demand for this second kit.

Thanks to Jack Ross for 15 years of encouragement; for wisdom, advice, and a helpful hand; for being a welcoming friend at teachers' conventions; and for being a saint over and over and over and over.

Thanks to Dick Buehler for providing American history perspectives, for once more attending the birth of a book and for being a loyal friend and sounding board.

Very special thanks to Elizabeth's daughter-in-law, Nadine Simms, for creating order out of a chaotic office; for finding Elizabeth's glasses again and again; for an exacting reading of the manuscript in its early stages; and for editing, cutting, pasting, photocopying, errands, and scrubbing vegetables, and for being an irreplaceable friend.

Thanks to Judy Markward of Word Perfect for midnight help on straightening out Elizabeth's screen when it went haywire.

Thanks to Gail Tyrrel, Tom D'Aquanni, Eilene Mething, and many others at Landmark Education Corporation for inspiration and training in mind management.

Thanks to the River Edge Schools' Bilingual Parent Volunteers, past and present, who have contributed tirelessly to Judie's ESL program.

Very special thanks to Judie's sons Charles and Joe, and her friend Karen Gloster, who all helped her create the very first Learning Centers and Starter Packs.

Last, we'd like to acknowledge each other for having the same commitments to ESL students and mainstream teachers, for having the same energies and faults, and for easily understanding and forgiving each other. This all possibly stems from our having the same birthday, and it might have been destined that we work together.

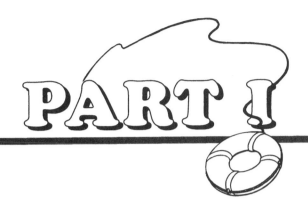

PART I

Teacher's Guide

1

About This Kit

The response to *Classroom Teacher's ESL Survival Kit #1* was far beyond our expectations, and we have been deluged with requests from ESL and mainstream teachers for more reproducible activity pages. To satisfy those requests, we have created *Classroom Teacher's ESL Survival Kit #2.* Here you will find 165 pages of self-checking, language-building activities for students at beginning and low-intermediate levels of English in grades three through eight.

The black line masters in this book may be reproduced for your own classes as you need them. The pages are three-hole-punched, and perforated so they can be stored conveniently in a three-ring binder.

Answer keys are provided on pages A1–A15. If you reproduce them, students can correct their own work, or a peer tutor can correct it.

Part One of the text contains the Teacher's Instructions for the Reproducible Activity Pages. You will find objectives for each activity and a variety of ways to use it. Some of the activities will be obvious; the Teacher's Instructions will help you discover additional activities. Compare notes with other teachers at your grade level. Read through the general instructions first to make most effective use of the reproducibles.

Part Two contains the black line masters in five sections: school scenes, easy stories, math, science, and social studies. At the bottom of each Activity Sheet is a reference to the page where you can find instructions for using it.

A. The School Scenes section contains full-page illustrations of various classrooms. Each illustration has a short text describing the actions going on in the scene; there are 30 possible language-building activities for each scene.

B. The Stories section has easy, illustrated Aesop's stories with 20 possible activities per story.

C. The Science section has four units. The first is a cut-and-paste unit working with animal vocabulary and classification. The other units include weather (which is apt to be different from that in the student's native country), temperature (the Fahrenheit scale is new to many ESL students), and flowering plants.

D. The Math section focuses on the language used when talking about numbers and math concepts. Practice is provided with coins, dollars, and counting money, and with measurement systems (pounds and ounces, feet and inches, cups, pints, quarts and gallons). These systems are new and seem irrational to students who have grown up with the metric system of measurement in other parts of the world.

5. The <u>Social Studies</u> section presents basic facts about the United States that English-speaking students in grade five are apt to know already. Illustrated readings and activities introduce the geography, early history, government, leaders, and symbols of the United States.

Classroom Teacher's ESL Survival Kit #2 is designed to follow *Classroom Teacher's ESL Survival Kit #1*. In *Kit #1*, you will find a 65-page teacher's manual with suggestions for:

- helpful district policies

- advance preparations for new arrivals

- insights into student culture shock

- first day check list

- strategies for communicating and building self-esteem

- hundreds of practical ideas and teaching tips

- information about ESL students and their learning styles

- strategies for helping ESL students read English

- ways of multiplying your limited time with ESL students

- tips on modifying assignments

In addition, *Kit #1* contains 120 black-line reproducible masters for:

- teacher tools

- diagnostic and observation forms

- a welcome booklet

- school-orientation pages

- letter-matching activities

- and more than a hundred language-building activities

2

Meeting the Needs of the ESL Students

No classroom teacher has the time to do a tenth of what is needed by ESL students. But relax: clone yourself. Use mainstream students as peer teachers to help with the newcomers. This can work out well for you, for the native-English speakers, and for the newcomers. Interacting with and helping others is a basic life skill and is never a waste of a student's time. The experience of being a "deputy teacher" may be one of the most powerful learning experiences your native speakers have in their school career. Peer teachers will multiply your efforts and provide age-level social support. They need some orientation and guidance from you, and acknowledgment from you and the school for the very special contributions they can make. See *Kit #1*, pages 3-7 for tips in this area.

Students learning in a new language need daily opportunities for success in order to fuel their motivation in the face of the hundreds of inevitable frustrations and failures to understand.

They also need a positive relationship with a caring adult (you) to help them summon the courage to risk expression in a new language.

For at least part of each day, include your newcomers in your mainstream lessons; have them work with a buddy or in a sociable group. Supplement your presentations with plenty of visuals to capture their attention. Let them "get a feel for the water"–but not be drowned by too-early immersion. Thirty to sixty minutes spread throughout the day might be the maximum for beginning students in the middle elementary grades. The brain tunes out when there is more input than it can handle, and then time is wasted.

For other parts of the day, allow newcomers to progress at their own individual rates in activities that are more closely geared to their language abilities.

Also, allow students who are literate in their own language to spend time writing in a native-language journal, or writing home to family and friends in their native countries. This heightens their observation of the new surroundings and enables them to express the myriad feelings that being in a novel environment generates. Many children gain a sense of support from being able to confide in someone who understands, even if that person is 12,000 miles away. Provide an envelope and appropriate airmail postage so the transaction can be completed. (Have the child's parent address the envelope.) Students may also keep a journal to take home and share with parents, or keep for themselves.

Entry-level students need to hear the sounds of the printed words in the materials in this kit. If possible, you, an aide, a mainstream student, or a volunteer might read materials to the students. Another option is to record the materials on audio cassettes. A recording multiplies your efforts because the students can listen to the tape as many times as needed. The recording can be used with many different students. Supply a comfortable set of headphones so the students may listen without disturbing the rest of the class. (Don't, however, neglect the ESL students' need for interaction with real speakers. Headphones can isolate learners from others: balance is needed.) The recordings should be at a slow-normal pace, with sufficient pause at the end of each sentence to allow the students to mentally connect the picture, text and the sounds of the language. Instruct your students in the use of the pause button on the cassette player. Label all recordings completely, and maintain in appropriate containers. See *Kit #1*, page 6, for more tips for making, duplicating, identifying, storing and using audio recordings.

Intermediate ESL students who are able to read can do many of the activities without audio assistance, but it is still advisable to at least pronounce the new words in the word box for them.

Vary a day's assignments to include work from more than one subject in several different learning modes: listening, reading, copying, guided writing, coloring, drawing, tracing, cutting and pasting, matching, playing, rote memorization, doing puzzles, research, native language reading and writing, plus interactive tasks and hands-on activities.

Time spent reading *in any language* is well spent. ESL students should read in their native language each day, in order to maintain their reading skills, many of which will be transferable. If possible, supply native-language books or magazines from the media center, or get some

on loan from a larger library. If the students can bring suitable materials from home, so much the better.

Students may spend time drawing pictures of their country to share with classmates. Assign them to draw their school, their classroom, their friends, teachers, home, street, pets, and so forth.

Have students copy pictures, maps, tables, and charts from their new mainstream textbooks, practice handwriting skills, listen to taped lessons, browse through picture books, do assignments from this book, and do their ESL homework.

Students who are skilled in rote-memorization (as newcomers may be) can increase self-esteem through memorizing easily understood and clearly useful matters such as state locations on a map, capitals, short poems, proverbs, songs, tongue-twisters, facts, and dates. Give them short chunks at a time. Demonstrating this kind of competence will help them maintain a sense of participation and progress.

Students from countries that have different writing systems will need some individual help to learn letter formation, and a lot of practice before they can write neatly. A neat paper is a source of pride, regardless of the content, so provide time and encouragement for handwriting practice.

Each student in grade three and up needs his or her own copy of a bilingual dictionary. If parents don't provide dictionaries, ask the media center to order a quantity of them in appropriate languages so each ESL student may borrow a dictionary for the year. If the students don't know how to use a dictionary, ask parents to teach them, or have bilingual personnel teach them dictionary skills. Allow beginning students to use their dictionaries freely to verify new vocabulary.

3

Managing and Keeping Track of ESL Students Effort and Progress

Delegate preparation, photocopying, instruction, and correction tasks wherever possible so you can use your limited time most effectively to encourage and acknowledge the students' work.

You do not need to work from the beginning of the book to the end. Omit sections that are not applicable to your students' needs or abilities.

Photocopy the materials, three-hole punch them, and staple them along the left margin into booklets of a manageable length. Distribute to your ESL students as needed.

Photocopy the answer sheets so classmates may check the ESL students' work, or the students may self-correct.

Photocopy plenty of the Daily Schedule Sheets (*Kit #1*, Page R30). Show students how to plan their time on a daily basis. This may have to be done initially through an interpreter, but the investment of time early on will make light years of difference over the school term and can cut in half the time needed to make an academic adjustment. Make students aware that although they may not be able to understand your lessons for the class, and won't be required to do the assignments other students are doing, all of their time is valuable and is to be used in as productive a way as possible.

Photocopy plenty of the Keeping Track Sheets (Page R1). The tracking sheets will help ESL students document their efforts and help you to see at a glance the quantities of work being accomplished. Show the students how to enter the date, page, and activity in the appropriate columns. Each activity page offers possibilities for several language skills, so each can be used several times. Indicate by *U, R, S,* or *W* (Understanding, Reading, Speaking, or Writing) which of the skills the students have practiced. Have the ESL students sit with you for a few minutes a day to review their progress after their work has been either self-corrected or peer-corrected. Set standards and challenges; acknowledge their efforts. Initial the final column when the activity has been completed. Give constant encouragement. When Tracking Sheets are filled, you can include them in the student's portfolio assessment folders. You can also photocopy them as part of a report to parents.

4

Helping ESL Students Learn New Vocabulary

Vocabulary is presented in a context of a description of a scene, or a story, or matched with an illustration. In many of the activities, important words are placed in a key word list or word box.

Depending on age and language ability, have students do one or more of the following activities with the new words.

- Listen to a peer or a recording of the vocabulary in context or accompanied by its illustration.

- Point to the illustration of the spoken word.

- Write the meanings of the words in their own language.

- Find and underline the words in the reading selection.

- Make a picture dictionary of the words

- Copy the words several times each.

- Alphabetize the words.

- Write the words in individual sentences.

- Select five or ten words for their personal spelling list that they will study for a test by you or a peer teacher.

- Utilize the game formats below to encourage interaction and to add fun to the learning.

- Cut 3" by 5" index cards in half and use them for matching games. Make flash cards with the word on one side and a picture or native language word on the other.

- Have students write a vocabulary word on one card, and a corresponding picture or native language word on a matching card. Students may play Scramble, Pick Up or Concentration with the cards.

Scramble: (a solitaire game): Spread all the cards out on the student's desk. Racing against the clock, the student must pick up the cards in matched pairs.

Double Scramble: Two or more students compete with each other to find matched pairs. (This version gets noisy.)

Pick Up: Spread the picture cards out on the desk. A partner, peer teacher, or volunteer shuffles the word cards, then calls them one at a time. The student must locate the picture of the word called. The game may be played with the word cards on the table and student must locate the word that the teacher or partner calls out.

Crossword puzzles: Teach students strategies for completing puzzles if necessary. Help students notice that clues are given for each word: the written clue, the number of letters in the puzzle, and the letters filled in by the cross words. Let them see that they can skip difficult questions and return to them later when more of the puzzle has been filled in.

Word-search puzzles: Show students how to locate and circle the words from the word list that are hidden in the large square, and to write a check next to each word they have found.

- Refer to *Kit # 1* for additional games, interactive activities, and ways of making connections between newcomers and mainstream students.

Increasing And Decreasing the Level of Difficulty

To decrease difficulty: read the selections to the students at a pace comfortable for them, stopping to check comprehension as often as needed. To increase difficulty, have students listen to a recording of the material at a slow-normal pace. To further increase the difficulty, have the student read the selection with no audio support.

To increase difficulty in doing activities, you may have students cover the word box, or be restricted from referring back to the original text.

5

Instructions

A. Instruction for School Scenes
Pages R2–R27

Format: Each of the five scene units consists of a full-page illustration, a KEY WORDS box, a short text, a cloze exercise, a YES/NO or matching activity, and a puzzle. You can use the scenes for a variety of purposes.

Student objectives:

- to increase awareness of, and ease in, the new environment
- to learn terms for objects and activities in various school locations
- to understand and read descriptions in the present and present continuous tenses
- to respond to simple yes/no question forms
- to follow directions for multiple-choice, and cloze tests
- to learn how do to word puzzles
- to write simple sentences and a simple paragraph

Procedures for Specific Teacher Objectives

1. **To evaluate student aural comprehension:** Ask the new students to point to items or actions as you say them. Examples: "Point to a lunch bag. Point to a boy standing in line." "Are the children sitting at a table?"

2. **To evaluate student oral production:** Ask students to tell what they see in the illustration. Ask questions that will require short answers or longer phrases and sentences, depending on your students' language ability. Examples: "What is this?" "What is this girl carrying?" "Why are the children standing in line?" "What do you think will happen next?"

3. **To build relationship with the students:** Ask individual students questions about his or her likes, dislikes, abilities, possessions, feelings and experiences as they relate to the illustration. Examples: "What do you like to eat for lunch?" "Who do you sit with at lunch time?"

4. **To evaluate student writing skills:** Have the students label as many items in the scene as they can, then write sentences about what is happening in the picture and what they think will happen next.

5. **To teach new vocabulary and structures:** Help students learn the names of the characters in the scenes. These characters are repeated in all five scenes, and their names are a

clue to understanding the text. The girls are Akiko, Carmen, Jennifer, Mei, Nadia, and Shantra. The boys are Alain, Joe, Miguel, Palo, Po Wen, and Tan.

a. Read the text, or have a peer teacher read the text, as the students look at the scene. The reader should help the learners locate the character in the scene that each sentence refers to, and demonstrate the meaning of the verb.

b. Or have the students listen to a tape of the scene as they look at the picture. If you use a tape, allow the students to rewind it and listen to it as many times as needed.

c. Ask questions about the scene: "Who is doing homework?" "Who is drinking juice?" Have students point to the correct person, say the correct name, or answer in a sentence ("Jennifer is drinking juice."), depending on their ability.

6. **To stimulate student observation and art skills:** Ask the students to draw a picture of the corresponding room in your school, and to label objects, students, teachers. Have them write sentences about their picture.

7. **To enable students to share their native language:** Have students label the scene in their own language and share it with a buddy or small group. Post the labeled scenes around the classroom.

8. **To help students share their native culture:** Invite students to draw a picture of the corresponding classroom in their native country and show it to a buddy, a group or the class. Then ask the students questions about it. "Did you have a lunch room in your school in (native country)?" "Did you go home for lunch?" "Draw a picture of the place where you ate lunch."

9. **To help students follow directions and use fine motor skills:**

Have students color the illustration in accordance with any directions provided, or as they desire.

10. **To develop students' sight, sound, and meaning correspondences:** Have the ESL students read the "Look, listen and read" paragraph silently as you (or a classmate) read it aloud, pointing to words if necessary. The illustration should be visible for reference. Ask questions to which the students may locate the answers in the text: "Who is standing in line?" "What is Nadia carrying?"

11. **To develop student listening and speaking skills:** Have students read along while listening to a tape. They may press the pause button after each sentence and repeat the sentence. Listen, or have a classmate listen, as the student reads the paragraph aloud.

12. **To build students' vocabulary recognition and spelling:** Have students study the WORD BOX, then locate those words in the paragraph and underline them.

13. **To help students visualize meanings from aural input:** Read, or have a classmate read, as the students close their eyes.

14. **To enable students to practice letter formation, spelling, word spacing, punctuation, and fine motor skills:** Have students copy the paragraph. A classmate can check for accuracy.

15. **To develop students' speaking skills:** After they become familiar with the text, have students look at the illustration and tell in their own words what is happening.

16. **To develop students' vocabulary and spelling:** Have students write the missing words on the lines provided in the "Listen, read, and write" activity.

- To increase the level of difficulty, cover the word box before you copy the page for the students. Make two or three copies of the cloze exercise and have the students progress through the three stages of difficulty.

17. **To build students' auditory memory and spelling skills:** For an additional level of difficulty, dictate the entire paragraph, (or have the students listen to it on a tape cassette) and have students write it down.

18. **To build skill in writing complete sentences:** After the students have completed the above activities, have them look at the picture, write sentences about the scene from memory, then check their work against the text.

19. **To encourage creative and predictive thinking:** Invite the students to make other comments about the characters in the scene: "What will happen next?" "What are the characters talking about?" "How do they feel about what they are doing?" "Which ones are friends?" "Where do you think they are from?"

20. **To enable students to demonstrate their comprehension and to practice their artistic skills:** Have students read the sentences and "draw the pictures" to illustrate sentence meanings. Encourage their original drawings, rather than copying from the illustrations. Demonstrate stick figures if the students are frustrated by this activity.

How to Extend the Activities

Have a classmate take ESL students on a "guided tour" of each classroom, pointing out and naming specific items, and being sure the newcomers know the names of the different teachers they encounter, as well as the nurse, principal, school secretary, librarian, and so forth.

ESL students can cut pictures from magazines that relate to the illustrations. They might paste them in a booklet with labels (for example, foods with the lunchroom scene, body parts with the nurse's office scene). You might want to use a page of a picture dictionary in conjunction with various scenes. For example, they can learn additional food vocabulary with the lunchroom scene so they can talk about food likes and dislikes.

B. Instructions for Easy Stories:
Pages R28–R49

Format: Each unit consists of the text for a story, a page of illustrations with word balloons indicating what the characters might be saying; a KEY WORDS box, a cloze exercise, a yes/no or a matching activity, and a puzzle. More than 20 different activities may be done with each unit.

Student Objectives

- to enjoy stories
- to build vocabulary through whole-language in meaningful contexts
- to build sight-reading skills and phonics in context
- to build aural comprehension
- to retell a story in one's own words

Procedures for Specific Teacher Objectives

1. **To foster sound/meaning correspondence:** Read (or have a peer, aide, or volunteer read) the stories to the students or have students listen to the story on a tape cassette. Have them look at the illustrations while listening.

2. **To build sound/symbol correspondence skills:** Have students listen to the story while following along in the text. If you have made a tape recording, the students may rewind the tape and listen to it as many times as desired, having both text and illustrations in front of them.

3. **To check student comprehension, "Fill in the Correct Box."** Have students read the questions and select the best answer. They may refer back to the text to check their work. They may copy the completed sentences on another sheet of paper.

4. **To encourage listening for and recalling missing words:** Use the "Listen, read, and write" page. Have students listen to the story on tape, or have a buddy or volunteer read it to them. Have students write in the missing words. For intermediate students, no audio may be necessary. For more advanced students, or for a second go-round, cover the word box before photocopying the page.

5. **To focus students attention on sentence structure:** Use the scrambled sentences. (Pages R48-R49) Demonstrate the meaning of scrambled by changing the word order in a short sentence. Example: "I speak English." ("speak English I.") Demonstrate how each group of words on the page may be rearranged to create a sentence from the story they have recently read.

6. **To provide practice in penmanship, spelling, and the mechanics of writing:** Have students copy the story.

7. **To provide practice in oral reading skills:** Have students read the story aloud to another student.

8. **To encourage students' speaking skills:** Listen as students retell the story in their own words while looking at the pictures.

9. **To encourage thinking and writing skills:** Have students write in the word balloons what they think the characters in the story are thinking or saying.

10. **To encourage original thinking and creative writing:** Have students create a different story for the same illustrations, or have them add to or change the illustrations and create a new story. Or have them write a similar story, with different animal characters.

11. **To check students' spelling:** Ask a classmate to give the ESL students a spelling test or dictation based on the story.

12. **To stimulate critical thinking and analysis:** Ask students to tell or write what lesson the story teaches. For example: Get ready for the winter while it is still summer (work when you are young so you will have a home to live in when you are old).

C. Instructions for Science: Pages R50–R75

Provide materials for observation and manipulation. For example, provide magnifying glasses and allow students to observe and draw insects; have them chart the weather (See R56–R67), plant seeds (R68–R75), and so forth.

1. Animal Concepts:
Pages R50–R55 (Cut and Paste)

Format: Six pages of animal pictures invite students to categorize animals by cutting and pasting them in appropriate rows or columns.

Student Objectives:

- to learn vocabulary for a wide variety of animals

- to learn various ways in which animals are classified, including distinctions between farm and zoo; farm animals, bugs, water animals, wild animals; animals and their babies; how animals move; animal skin coverings; animal eating habits

- to develop fine-motor skills through cutting and pasting

General Procedures

- Provide scissors and glue or paste, or transparent tape.
  Note: Students who have had little schooling may need extra time to practice with scissors and paste.

- Point to and name the animals as the students listen.

- Have the students point to each animal as you say the names at random.

- Have students say the names of the animals.

- Have students cut out the animals and glue them in the correct places.

- Encourage students to color the animals, referring to a picture dictionary or other source for accurate colors.

- Have students copy each animal name at least once.

- Have students write a short sentence for each animal. Examples: "A horse lives on a farm," "A bee can fly," "A chicken has feathers."

- Have students divide a blank page into several columns or sections similar to the activity they have just completed. Have them write a label in each section and draw pictures of other animals that fit into each category. Have them label their pictures, using a picture dictionary or a bilingual dictionary if needed.

Additional Animal Activities

- Have students browse through picture books to look for unfamiliar animals and their names.

- Have students read easy-to-read books about animals. Have them do a simple book report on an animal book of their choice.

- Have students draw pictures of animals they are familiar with, animals in their native countries, or their own pet.

2. Weather: Pages R56–R67
Overall Objectives:

- to have students become familiar with the Fahrenheit scale

- to read a thermometer

- to learn English expressions connected with temperatures

- to notice differences in weather patterns in their new environment

- to learn the English expressions for weather phenomena

- to understand and write present, future and past expressions about the weather

What's the Temperature?
Page R56–R589

Objectives: To learn about and compare the Fahrenheit and the Celsius thermometers; the language of temperature measurement; boiling and freezing points of water, and normal body temperature and indications of fever on the Fahrenheit scale.

Procedures:

- Read the material to the students or have them listen to a cassette recording as many times as needed. Help them understand that the symbol "º" is read "degrees".

- Provide a small thermometer for hands-on observation. Have another thermometer outside a classroom window.

- Newcomers are likely to be familiar with the Celsius (Centigrade) scale, and will need experience with the Fahrenheit scale.

- Demonstrate how to write the temperatures in words. Have students notice that the symbol F represents *Fahrenheit*.

- Obtain several ice cubes and place them in a glass of water. Place the thermometer in it and have the students observe the movement of the column of alcohol. Have students note what happens when the thermometer is removed from the water; when the thermometer is held between their fingers or under their arms.

- Point out to the students that the thermometer reads only up to 110 degrees. (Do not attempt to heat the thermometer! Hot water would cause the glass to break as the column of alcohol expanded past 110 degrees.)

- To complete page R58, have students refer to indoor and outdoor thermometers in the classroom as well as to the previous text pages.

Page R59 is designed to help students distinguish between the words *hot, warm, cool,* and *cold*. (*Cool* and *warm* may be hard to distinguish by mere temperature designations. *Cool* refers to temperatures that are decreasing in comparison with previous temperatures, while *warm* refers to temperatures that are increasing in comparison with previous temperatures. Hence, in the spring, 60 degrees is warm, compared with winter, but in autumn, 60 is cool, compared with summer.) You don't need to be so technical. Call 70° warm and 50° cool.

What's the Weather?
Pages R60–R61

To teach the various expressions that describe the weather: "It's ____ing, and it's ____ y;" read the weather expressions to the students, or have the students listen to a tape.

Today's Weather: Page R62

To help students observe weather conditions and be able to describe and to write a paragraph about them, Give students at least five copies of this page. Each day have students observe the weather, check off their observations, and write five sentences about the day's weather.

Yesterday's Weather: Page R63

To prompt recall of the previous day's weather, and write a paragraph about it using the past tense, a day after completing page R62. have students check off the boxes for "Yesterday's Weather" on R62. (Point to yesterday on the calendar, if necessary.) Have them write, or copy, five sentences in the past tense about yesterday's weather.

My Weather Forecast: Page R64

To have students make a prediction about the next day's weather and write a paragraph using the future *will*, have students complete another copy of page R62. Then have them think about tomorrow's weather. (Point to the calendar to clarify *tomorrow* if necessary). Have them check the box next to the kind of weather they think will happen the next day. Then have them copy the five sentences about tomorrow's weather. The following day, have students compare their forecast with the actual weather. Continue for as many days as desired.

Keep a Weather Calendar:
Pages R65 and R66

To foster students' observing weather over a period of time, and using the past and superlative forms of weather expressions, have students observe the weather outdoors and keep a weather diary for two weeks. They can write the dates in each box on R66 and draw symbols for the weather they observe. Have them compute the total number of days of each type of weather. If desired, teach the students the names of the different kinds of clouds: *cumulus, cirrus, stratus, nimbus.*

Temperature Chart: Page R67

Procedures: Have students fill in the dates across the bottom of the page for the upcoming two weeks. Instruct them to read the outdoor thermometer at the same time each day, and to draw a dot on the graph to show the temperature for that day. If possible, have them record the temperature for the weekend, too. (Otherwise, leave two days blank for Saturday and Sunday. then they can draw lines connecting each day's temperature to the next and observe if there is a general trend of warming or cooling. Several copies of the chart and can be taped together for observations over a longer period of time.)

Extension: Have students look at a weather map of the nation and learn to read weather symbols. Ask questions such as "What's the weather in Boston?" "What's the temperature in Miami?" "Is it raining in Chicago?"

3. Plants Pages R68–R75

Student Objectives:

- to participate in a science project
- to learn the names of parts of a flowering plant and their functions
- to learn the process of fertilization
- to distinguish between fruits (seed bearing part of a plant) and vegetables
- to increase observational skills
- to appreciate nature

Parts of a Plant: Pages R68–R69
Procedures:

- Use a live flowering plant, if possible, to illustrate the reading. Read aloud the material on page R67 to the students, or have them read it. Point to the pictures or the parts of the live plant as you refer to them.

- Verify comprehension. Say: "Point to the roots." "Point to the stem." "Where do the roots get water from?" and so forth.

- Have students copy the text or the new vocabulary words. Have them draw an illustration for each word.

- Have students use each of the vocabulary words in a simple sentence. Examples: "Plants are green." "The pollen is on the stamen."

How Flowers Make Seeds:
Pages R71–R73

- If plants are available in the classroom, have the students draw pictures of them and label their parts using the words from the word box.

- Bring to class several flowers, or even realistic plastic flowers, and have students examine them to find the parts of a flower.

- Bring in a variety of fruits and vegetables. Cut them open and have students look for the presence or absence of seeds. If seeds are present, it is the fruit of the plant, even if we commonly call it a vegetable. Examples: peas, beans, squash, pepper, tomato, eggplant.

- Have students notice the symmetrical arrangement of seeds in an apple cut horizontally, in oranges, in lemons, and so forth.

- Provide soil and cups or pots so students may plant seeds and observe their growth. Have students measure the plants and keep a chart of the growth of the plant. Or have them draw a life-size picture of the plant each week.

D. Instructions for Math
Pages R76–R114

General Notes: Counting in one's native language is usually deeply ingrained, and even after 20 years in a new country, a person will revert to his or her native language when accuracy in computing is desired. Extensive practice is needed to achieve complete bilingual facility with numbers.

Student Objectives: to understand, read, and use the language needed for:

- counting
- talking about various kinds of numbers
- doing math operations
- reading simple word problems
- talking about money
- telling time
- the U.S. system of weights and measures.

Note: Select only the activity pages for math vocabulary and concepts that are introduced at or before the students' grade level.

On pages that present a list of terms, read or have a buddy read the terms to the students. Then read the terms at random and have the students point to the correct illustration or word. Have students copy the terms and symbols.

Write the Number Page R76

Objective: to understand, read and write the words for the numbers zero through ten thousand.

Procedures:

- Have students read the number words and fill in the answers.
- On a separate sheet of paper have students write the numbers you dictate. Repeat this activity until students gain a degree of automaticity with this.
- Spelling test. Have the students write the numbers on page R76 on a separate sheet of paper. Then, without looking at the original, have them spell the numbers. Then they can check their answers against the original.

Draw the Hands on the Clocks: Page R77

Objective: to understand and read simple statements about time.

Procedures: Review numbers through 60. Have students practice counting by fives. Work with both a digital clock or watch and a cardboard "conventional clock" with movable hands. Move the minutes on the digital clock and help students to say the times.

- Have students read the time statements under each clock and draw the hands.
- Statements about time using the more complex patterns, (It's twenty minutes after five; It's ten to three, and so forth) can be introduced to more advanced students. The pages may be used again with these new structures if desired.

What Time Is It? Page R78

Objective: to write time statements.

Procedures: Have students write the statement about the time under each clock.

- On a separate sheet of paper, have students draw additional clocks, draw in the hands, and write time statements about the clocks.

Math Symbols: Page R79

Objective: to understand and learn the names of common math symbols.

Procedures: See general instructions for teaching vocabulary, page 8.

- Have students use numbers and symbols to write the indicated sentences.

Read and Write with Math Symbols : Page R80

Objective: to practice the language of numerical expressions.

Procedures: Have students read each numerical expression aloud as you listen. Then have them write the expressions in words.

The Multiplication Table: Page R81

Objective: To increase facility with number words; to review the multiplication tables; to practice the verbal expressions for multiplying.

Procedures: Demonstrate that this table is created by multiplying the number running down the left side of the table by the numbers running across the top of the table.

- Have students complete the table where there are missing figures.

- Ask questions such as "How much is three times six?" Have students provide just the answer at first, then a complete sentence with an answer. Then have the students read and write the answers to the questions.

U. S. Coins and Bills: Page R82

Objective: to learn names, appearances and values of American coins.

Procedures: Use actual coins if available to teach the names (penny, nickel, dime, quarter, half dollar, dollar) and their values. Be sure the students can recognize the coins from the tails side as well as head side. American coins do not have the value printed on them, and the five cent piece is larger than the ten cent piece, which is confusing to younger children.

- Have students copy the names of coins.

- Teach intermediate students the names of the presidents pictured on the coins.

How Much Is It? Page R83

Objective: to practice calculating the value of groups of coins.

Procedures: On a table or desk, using real money or facsimile money, create groups of coins such as three nickels, two dimes and a penny, etc., and have the students calculate the total value. Then have the students calculate the values on the activity sheet.

Read and Write About Money: Page R84

Objective: to understand, read and write about quantities of money.

Procedures: Help students read the money expressions. Show them that there is more than one correct way. Then have them write the money expressions in words.

- Dictate various money amounts to the students and have them write them on a separate sheet of paper. Example: thirty-two cents; a dollar and twenty nine cents; a dollar fifty; a eighty-five cents; two-eighty five; three forty-nine.

Solve These Word Problems: Page R85–R88

Objective: to understand and read simple word problems and learn key phrases that indicate which operation is needed.

Procedures: Have students read the word problems; point out the words that indicate which operation is needed.

- Have students write the answers.
- Have students copy the word problems.
- Have students create their own word problems with pictures to illustrate them.

Read the Numbers: Ordinals: Page R89

Objective: to understand, read and write ordinal numbers.

Procedures: See General Instructions for teaching vocabulary

- Have students read and write the answers in complete sentences following the model sentence. Extend the concept to other familiar groupings in the classroom: students in rows; days of the week; months of the year; subjects in the day; grades in school.

Place Values: Pages R90–R91

Objective: to learn the vocabulary and expressions needed to talk about the concept of place value; to understand, read and write large numbers; to know where to place a comma to separate thousands. (Be aware that confusion can arise since in South America and elsewhere, commas are used to indicate the decimal, and a period is used where we use a comma. Some Asian counting systems place a comma every four digits, rather than every three digits.) Give the students lots of practice in reading large numbers aloud.

Procedures: Read the examples with the students. Ask the students to write additional examples of one, two, three and four digit numbers.

- Point out that the comma in the four digit number says "thousand."
- Point out that when writing the year, 1996, for example, no comma is used, and it is read nineteen ninety six. (Activity R93 gives additional practice.)
- Have the students complete the pages, and correct their own answers.

How to Read Large Numbers: Page R92

Objective: to learn the English needed to read large numbers

Procedures: Point out that the comma, as you move to the left, says "thousand," then "million," then "billion," and "trillion."

- Have students read the numbers aloud.

Read and Write Large Numbers: Page R93

Objective: to increase facility with reading and writing large numbers.

Procedures: Have students place commas where needed and read the numbers aloud.

- Have students write the words for the numbers, using an additional sheet of paper if needed.
- Dictate additional large numbers for the students to write. Have them place commas in the correct places.

Different Ways of Reading Numbers: Page R94

Objective: to become aware that numbers are not always read in the same way, that their use determines their reading.

Procedures: Point out to students that numbers on doors and in addresses and in telephone numbers are not read the same way as they are in counting. (Telephone numbers in South America may be read in two-digit combinations.)

Math Terms: Page R95

Objective: to learn common math terms

Procedures: Have students read the examples and complete the activities.

Different Kinds of Numbers
Page R96

Objective: to learn the terms cardinal, ordinal, Arabic, Roman, even and odd numbers, fractions, decimals, mixed numbers, negative numbers and unknown numbers.

Procedures: (see general instructions for teaching vocabulary, page 8.) Have students study the illustrated examples and complete the matching activity.

Fractions –1: Page R97

Objective: to understand, read and write the terms for various fractions.

Procedures: Read the names of the fractional terms to the students. Call out the names at random, and have the students point to the correct fraction.

- Have students complete the activity, and read their work to you.

Fractions –2: Page R98

Objective: to understand, read and write the vocabulary of simple fraction operations.

Procedures: Read the terms to the students.

- Dictate terms for the students to write such as: a fraction with the numerator 4 and the denominator 5, etc.

- Have students match the fractions that have common denominators.
- Have them write additional fractions with common denominators.

Decimal Numbers: Page R99

Objective: to understand and read the words for decimal numbers.

Procedures: Read the terms to the students. Have students read the terms.

- Dictate several decimal terms for the students to write: three tenths; seven tenths, two and four tenths; five hundredths; seven and eleven hundredths; etc.
- Have students complete the exercise.

Lines: Page R100

Objective: to understand, read and write the names of various kinds of lines.

Procedures: See general instructions for teaching vocabulary, page 8.

- Have students draw the correct lines in the spaces provided.

Angles and Triangles: Page R101

Objective: to read and understand terms with angles and triangles.

Procedures: Have students copy the pictures and the labels.

Shapes: Page R102

Objective: to learn the names of various plane and solid geometrical shapes.

Procedures: Have the students draw the shapes and lines and copy the words.

Circles: Page R103

Objective: to learn various terms connected with circles.

Procedures: Teach the vocabulary, then call out terms for the student to illustrate.

● **Draw the Shape or Line:**
Page R104

Objective: to demonstrate knowledge of terms for shapes and lines

Procedures: Demonstrate that students are to draw the shapes.

How Long Is This Pencil?
Page R105

Objective: to understand statements such as "the ___ is ___ inches long," and to say and write such statements.

Procedures: Have students look at the chart. Have them look at the pencil and tell them, the pencil is five inches long. How long is the ruler? Ask them about each item, and help them to make the statement, "the ___ is ___ inches long." Have the students complete the written activity.

● **How Tall Are These People?**
Page R106

Objective: to understand and read a chart; to understand such statements as "___ is ___ feet, ___ inches tall," and be able to say and write such statements.

Procedures: Ask "How tall is Joe?" Help students note the measuring stick at the left and answer. Ask about each person. When the students can answer the questions orally, have them complete the written activity.

Long, Wide, and High: Page R107

Objective: to learn the vocabulary long, wide, high, and to understand and state sentences such as: "The ___ is ___ inches long, ___ inches wide, and ___ inches high."

Procedures: Students from most other countries need practical hands-on practice with our measuring system. Show the students how to read a ruler and measure several items with the students.

• Measure a small box. Stress the terms, long, wide and high. Have the students look at the picture and notice the dimensions of the box. Ask them "How long is the box?" "How wide is the box?" "How high is the box?" Then have the students measure other items in the classroom to complete the activity.

• Show students how to read a ruler, with fractions of an inch. Have them measure assorted items on their desks or in the classroom. They should write the name of the item, and the measurements in the correct column. Then they can write sentences about the measurements of the item.

My Measurements Page R108

Objective: to become aware of self-measurements, and be able to state and write that "My ___ is ___ inches (feet) long (around.)". "I am ___ feet, ___ inch(es) tall."

Procedures: Have students use a tape measure to measure their height, and assorted body parts. Allow students to work in pairs.

Change Feet to Inches:
Page R109

Objective: to understand, read, state and write inch-feet-yard equivalences.

Procedures: Give students a yardstick and foot rulers to work with. Have them discover how many feet are in one yard, and how many inches are in a yard. Teach them the abbreviations for these terms. Have them complete the written activity.

• Teach the term yard and yard/ feet/inch equivalents as needed.

Measuring Liquid Page R110 – R111

Objective: to understand, read and state the vocabulary for liquid measurements, and the abbreviations used for these; to understand, state, and write the equivalences for teaspoon, tablespoon, ounces, cups, quarts, gallons.

Note: These units of measurement are quite different from the trouble-free metric system the students may be familiar with. If there is a way to give students some hands-on practice with them, take advantage of it.

Procedures: Provide the students with a gallon, a half gallon, two quarts, four cups, and assorted measuring spoons. Label each container and teach the names.

- If possible, allow students to work at a sink, if you have one in your classroom, or outdoors in a sandpile if one is available and the weather permits. (It's neater if you send the items home in a shopping bag and let the students work at home.) Instruct students to pour water from quart into cups, quarts into gallons.

You might ask students to:

- count the tablespoons of water in a cup.
- draw their own chart, using the containers they have been working with.
- copy the table of equivalences, then complete the written activities.

How Much Do These Things Weigh? – 1
Page R113

Objective: to learn the vocabulary for weight, and the English needed to say "the __ weighs __ (pounds.) To learn the equivalences of these terms, and the abbreviations for the terms.

Procedures: If you can bring in a bathroom scale for students to weigh them-

selves and classmates and heavier objects, do so.

- Provide the students with a postage or classroom scale if possible to weigh items such as books and pencils.
- Point out that an English gram is not the same as the gram in the metric system.
- Ask, How many ounces are in two pounds? How many pounds are in two tons?

How Much Do These Things Weigh? - 2 Page R114

Objective: to develop a sense of U.S. weights; to have a hands-on experience with using a small scale.

Procedures: Have students guess the weight of an item then weigh it on and record the weight on the chart on page 45. Then have them write sentences about the weights.

E. Instructions for Social Studies
Pages R115 - R161

General Notes

We have noticed that newcomers' most difficult subject is often American social studies. They have very little frame of reference for American geography and history, compared to science and math, which carry over from their studies in their native countries. They have to catch up with their American classmates who have been experiencing U. S. culture, and recent history all of their lives; native-born Americans may have lived in or traveled to other states; they have seen American movies and TV shows all their lives, and have had three or four years of cumulative school knowledge of American land, people, and history. American students' parents are more likely to be able to explain government, geography and history concepts to them, whereas newcomers' parents may be as much in the dark about U.S. history and geography as the newcomers themselves are.

The social studies materials in this kit attempts to fill in some of this basic knowledge. It highlights the major places, events, people, government, and concepts that are common knowledge to many third grade students, and to most fifth or sixth grade students in the United States. Select only the pages containing information expected to be known at your grade level in your school.

Format: There are three sections: Land and People, Early History, and Government. In all three sections, presentation pages of illustrated facts and concepts alternate with practice pages of vocabulary work and activities to help digest the language.

Objectives: to introduce basic facts in U.S. geography and history; to familiarize students with a U.S. map; to learn the names of the continent, neighbors, states, major rivers, mountains, lakes; to build vocabulary and concepts in U.S. social studies; to think about rights and responsibilities as citizens; to know the names of prominent Americans before 1800.

General Procedures: Read or record the presentation pages for students, or have them read the pages on their own. Demonstrate that they are to write the key words in their native language; they can find them in a bilingual dictionary. Have them reread the text and underline the key words. Have them do the practice activities three ways, at different times: First by being allowed to check the previous page for an answer, then by hearing a dictation of the exercise and filling in the missing words; then having to recall the answer.

There is a list of topics at the bottom of activity pages. Students may increase their stockpile of concepts about the United States by doing "visual research" in the media center, browsing through picture books, seeing filmstrips, and reading easy readers on the topics. Have students write a report of their work by filling in the Report R164.

Where Is the United States of America? Pages R115–R116

Objectives: to locate the United States and its neighbors on the North American continent; to learn the bodies of water that touch the United States.

Procedure: Provide a globe and help students locate their native country, and locate North America and the United States.

- Call out the place names for student to point to on the globe.

- Help students also to locate the north and south poles, equator, the continents and oceans.

The Fifty States Pages R117–R118

Objectives: To learn simple facts about the fifty states.

Procedure: Have students work with a variety of maps of North America, the globe, and a map of the states.

- Have students trace the map to get a feel for the shape of the country.

The Map of the United States Page R119–R122

Objectives: to introduce the names of the states and their locations; to learn the terms for the compass directions; to practice writing the names of the states.

The States and their Capitals Page R123

Objective: to become aware of the names of the fifty states and their capitals

Procedures: Encourage students to work in pairs calling out the state names and locating them on a map.

- Provide a blank map of the states, and have students label the states.

- Have students memorize the capitals of your state and the states that touch your state. Ambitious students may want to memorize all the capitals. Give special recognition for this remarkable feat.

United States Word Search
Page R124

Objective: to locate the names of 50 states in a puzzle; to become more familiar with the spelling of the names of the states.

Procedures: A list of state names is on page R123. Show students how to locate the words in the puzzle and circle them, checking them off on the list. The words are written across and down.

The United States: Land and Water Pages R125 - R126

Objective: to learn the names of major physical features of the United States

Procedures: On a physical map, point out the major features of the land of the United States.

- What mountains, rivers, lakes or other special features are in your state?

The United States Map Quiz
Page R127

Procedures: After completing the activity and checking their answers, students may write sentences using the cues provided. Example: North America is a continent.

The People of the United States
Pages R128–R129

Objective: to learn basic facts about the people of the United States.

Procedures: In addition to reading the page and learning the vocabulary, have students browse through photography books of the various faces of Americans, such as *A Day in the Life of the United States*.

The Leaders of the United States
Pages R130–R131

Objective: to learn the titles and names of the president and vice president of the United States; to be introduced to the concept of elections, and democratic form of government.

Procedures: Before you photocopy the page, paste pictures of the current president and vice president of the United States in the appropriate panels. Teach their names to the students.

Symbols of the United States
Pages R132–R133

Objective: To learn the names and appearances of famous symbols of the United States.

Procedures: Provide additional pictures of these symbols.

- Provide a tape recording of "The Star Spangled Banner", and a copy of the words.

- Show the eagle on various coins— the half dollar and quarter, and in the great seal.

My State Page R134

Objective: to become familiar with one's own state, its neighbors, governor, symbols and outstanding physical features.

Procedure: Provide a map of your state for the students to trace and label.

- Have them complete the sentences by looking at the map or asking a classmate. Have them learn significant geographical features of your state, with population, capital, industries, neighboring states, nickname, and so forth.

- Optional: have them learn the state bird, state flower, state motto.

My Town Page R135

Objectives: to become familiar with one's own town, its location on a map, mayor, and some interesting facts.

Procedure: Have the students fill in the information with the help of a classmate if possible.

- Provide a local map and have the students locate their street, the school location, and the location of various places such as the police department, fire station, post office, city hall, hospitals, churches, etc.

Early American History
Pages R136–R152

Objectives: To learn salient facts about Native Americans; to learn about explorers, and the settlement of the colonies of Spain, France and England in North America; to learn a cause of the American Revolution; to learn of the Declaration of Independence, the Constitution; to learn facts about George Washington and Thomas Jefferson.

Procedure: Have students read, or listen to each section.

- Many of the key words are abstract and cannot be illustrated; have students use their bilingual dictionaries.

Early American History Quiz
Page R153

Procedure: Have students complete the quiz and check their own answers.

- Have students create complete sentences by copying the matched beginnings and endings.

- Give the quiz again on a subsequent day to ascertain student knowledge, or give the quiz orally.

Early American History: Crossword Puzzle Page 154

Objectives: to recall words when their definitions are given; to review key words in American history; to enjoy the challenge of a puzzle.

Procedure: If necessary, show students how to locate the place where they are to write the answers to the clues. Give extra clues to get them started.

The Story of My Native Country
Page R155

Objectives: to relate the information being learned about the United States to the students' own native countries; to share information about one's native country: land, people, neighbors, capital, leader, and any special information.

Procedure: Have students illustrate as many concepts as possible about their own homelands, by drawing or tracing a map of their country, drawing pictures of their home, school, local occupations, trees, animals, flowers, foods. Display these in your room.

- Invite them to share that information with classmates.

The Three Branches of Government Pages R156 - R160

Note: The concepts on these pages are more abstract and should be delayed until the students have enough vocabulary and sufficient maturity to tackle them.

- If your own class holds elections for a class president, and sends representatives to a student council, and/or has a committee for resolving disagreements, this will help to illustrate the concepts involved.

The Three Branches of Government–5 Page R150

Objectives: to learn simple facts about the organization of the U.S. government: Congress, President and Supreme Court.

Procedures:

- Use newspaper headlines to illustrate functions of the different branches of government.

- Provide students with the names of the senators from your state and the representative from their districts.

- On page R158, have students write each word from the list in the correct column according to which branch of the government it refers to.

Americans Have Many Rights; Responsibilities Page R161–R162

Objectives: To learn some of the rights and responsibilities of Americans; to encourage good citizenship.

Procedures: Help students see the connection between rights and responsibilities. Have students list other rights they have. Have students ask their parents about rights in their native country and write about any rights they have in the United States that they did not have in their native country, or that they had in the native country but do not have here. (Example, they may not yet have the right to vote here, but they had that right in their own country.)

- Have students list additional responsibilities of school students. Example: Listen when others speak; participate in lessons; do homework.

Visual Research

It is vital that the students be helped to conceptualize more of the details and scenes of the United States. For this reason, we suggest you have them do "visual research." A list of topics is given in each section. Circle the ones you wish your students to do. Add any others you wish.

Ask the media center person at your school (or a classmate) to help the students find materials on these topics that are rich in visuals. Picture books, easy readers, *Time-Life Series* books, encyclopedias, videos, and filmstrips will help create references for many concepts the students are not able to read about in grade level materials.

Have students use the Report Form on page R165 to document their work. They can write about what they see or read, or draw pictures inspired by the book.

When students have gone through the topics touched on in the reproducible pages, they may continue visual research on other American topics. In the media center, show the students the sections containing U.S. geography and history, and biographies of U.S. heroes. Select books with good visuals. A student can either browse through quite a few books a day, or, select one book to examine more carefully to report on.

Slavery

- Eli Whitney and the cotton gin
- Life on the plantations
- Harriet Tubman, The Underground Railroad, Sojourner Truth
- Frederick Douglass, Nat Turner
- John Brown
- See video series, *Roots.*

The Civil War

- Abraham Lincoln
- The Confederacy, Robert E. Lee, Jefferson Davis
- Ulysses S. Grant
- See videos: *Gone With the Wind*; *Red Badge of Courage*

Moving West

- Lewis and Clark Expedition, Sacajawea
- Kit Carson, Davy Crockett, The Pioneers
- The California Gold Rush
- Texas, The War with Mexico, The Alamo
- The Indian Wars: Sequoia, The Trail of Tears, Tecumseh, Geronimo, Cochise, Sitting Bull, Custer; Wounded Knee
- See video *Dances With Wolves*

Inventors and Scientists

- Benjamin Franklin
- Eli Whitney and the cotton gin
- Robert Fulton and the first steamboat
- Alexander Graham Bell and the telephone
- Thomas Edison
- The Wright Brothers and the airplane
- George Washington Carver

Industrialists

- John Rockefeller, Claudius Vanderbilt, H.L. Harriman
- Huntington, Andrew Carnegie, Henry Ford

Activists for Human Rights

- Susan B. Anthony, Elizabeth Cady Stanton
- Lucretia Mott
- Elizabeth Blackwell
- Jane Addams, Clara Barton, Dorothea Dix
- Marcus Garvey, Paul Robeson

- Helen Keller
- Martin Luther King, Jr., Rosa Parks
- Robert Kennedy, Jimmy Carter
- Malcolm X, Jesse Jackson
- See video, *Eye on the Prize*

Presidents

- Abraham Lincoln
- Theodore Roosevelt
- Franklin D. Roosevelt
- John F. Kennedy
- Current president

America's Geographical Wonders

- The Grand Canyon
- Niagara Falls
- Yellowstone National Park
- Yosemite National Park
- The Lurray Caverns
- The Jersey Shore
- The Rocky Mountains
- The Great Lakes
- Carlsbad Caverns
- Death Valley
- The Badlands
- Glacier National Park

Important Places and Telephone Numbers Page R163

Objectives: To familiarize the students with essential community services; to know how to call the police, fire department, or call in sick to school.

Procedures: Help the students locate the information called for. Have them take the paper home and post it where the numbers will be available when needed. Have them memorize the numbers for police and fire.

Time Zones Page R164

Objectives: To notice the size of the United States: to realize that a phone call from New York to California must take the time difference into consideration. Point out that Alaska (not shown on the map) is one hour earlier than San Francisco; Hawaii is two hours earlier.

Procedures:. Have students read the text; have them figure the time differences between various cities. (When it's 5 o'clock in Chicago, what time is it in New York? In San Francisco? In Denver? etc.)

Weights and Measurements: Metric System and U.S. System
Page R164

Objectives: To provide a reference of equivalents between metric and U.S. system; to enable students to better understand values of U.S. weights and measures.

- Encourage students to use this sheet as a reference until they are familiar with American weights and measures. Don't require skill in conversions from one system to the other.

Report Page R165

Note: This report form is to enable students to participate in lessons, do book reports and visual research, and demonstrate effort. Make plenty of copies so your students can report on many books each week if desired.

- Show students where to find the information called for on the sheet. Demonstrate that they are to draw a picture, write as much as they can in English, or write a report in their native language.

PART II

Reproducible
Activity
Sheets

KEEPING TRACK

Page	Title	U, R, S, W	Ck. by	Date
____	_____	_____	_____	_____
____	_____	_____	_____	_____
____	_____	_____	_____	_____
____	_____	_____	_____	_____
____	_____	_____	_____	_____
____	_____	_____	_____	_____
____	_____	_____	_____	_____
____	_____	_____	_____	_____
____	_____	_____	_____	_____
____	_____	_____	_____	_____
____	_____	_____	_____	_____
____	_____	_____	_____	_____
____	_____	_____	_____	_____
____	_____	_____	_____	_____
____	_____	_____	_____	_____
____	_____	_____	_____	_____

See directions on page 7.

IN THE LUNCHROOM - 1

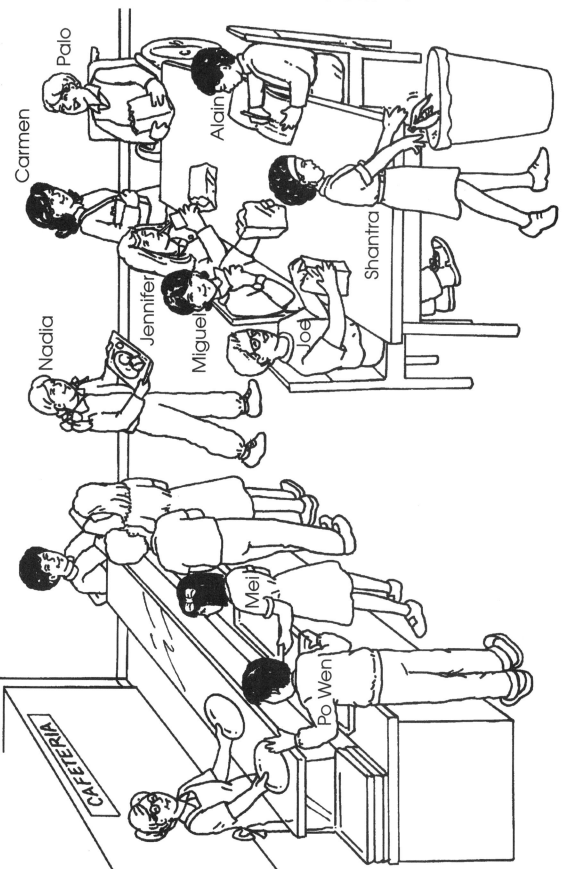

© 1995 by Elizabeth Claire and Barbara J. Haynes

IN THE LUNCHROOM - 2

I. Look, read and read.

This is a school lunchroom. Po Wen and Mei are standing in line. They are getting a school lunch. Nadia is carrying a tray to the table. Some students are at the table. Joe, Miguel, and Jennifer brought their lunches from home. Joe is opening his lunch bag. Miguel is eating a sandwich. He is talking to Joe. Jennifer is drinking juice. Palo is laughing with Carmen. Alain is doing homework. Shantra is throwing a banana peel in the garbage.

II. Match.

1. Nadia __G__   A. is opening his lunch bag.

2. Po Wen and Mei ____   B. is eating a sandwich.

3. Joe ____   C. are standing in line.

4. Alain ____   D. is throwing a banana peel in the garbage.

5. Miguel ____   E. is drinking juice.

6. Jennifer ____   F. is doing homework.

7. Palo and Carmen ____   ~~G~~. is carrying a tray.

8. Shantra ____   H. are laughing.

          See directions on page 10.

IN THE LUNCHROOM - 3

Listen, read, and write. Fill in the blank with a word from the box.

WORD BOX

laughing	standing	sandwich	lunch	carrying	opening
brought	homework	juice	throwing	garbage	

This is a school lunchroom. Po Wen and Mei are _____

in line. They are getting a school _____. Nadia is

_____ a tray to the table. Some students are at the

table. Joe, Miguel, and Jennifer _____ their lunches

from home. Joe is _____ his lunch bag. Miguel is

talking to Joe. He is eating a _____. Jennifer is

drinking _____. Palo is _____ with

Carmen. Alain is doing _____. Shantra is

_____ a banana peel in the_____.

IN THE LUNCHROOM - 4

Clothing Words

jeans	bow	sweatshirt	cardigan sweater
belt	vest	headband	sweatpants
purse	jacket	turtleneck sweater	sneakers

I. Color the picture of the students in the lunchroom. (Lightly)

a. Po Wen's jeans are blue.

b. Carmen's purse is tan.

c. Mei's bow is pink.

d. Palo's vest is red.

e. Joe's sneakers are white.

f. Nadia's sweatpants are purple.

g. Alain's turtleneck is green.

h. Shantra's headband is orange.

i. Shantra's belt is brown.

j. Jennifer's cardigan is yellow.

k. Po Wen's sweatshirt is gray.

l. Nadia's jacket is black.

II. Choose clothing from the list and draw a picture of yourself wearing it. Label the clothes in your picture.

   See directions on page 10.

Name _____ Date _____

IN THE LUNCHROOM - 5

Draw a picture to go with each sentence.

1. Two students are standing in line.

2. A girl is drinking juice.

3. A girl is carrying a tray.

4. A boy is eating a sandwich.

5. A boy is opening his lunch bag.

6. A girl is throwing garbage away.

IN THE LUNCHROOM - 6

Draw a picture of each word.

tray	juice	turtleneck sweater
banana peel	vest	standing
laughing	cardigan sweater	bowl
purse	lunch bag	sitting
garbage	sweatshirt	belt

  See directions on page 10.

Name _____ Date _____

IN THE LIBRARY - 1

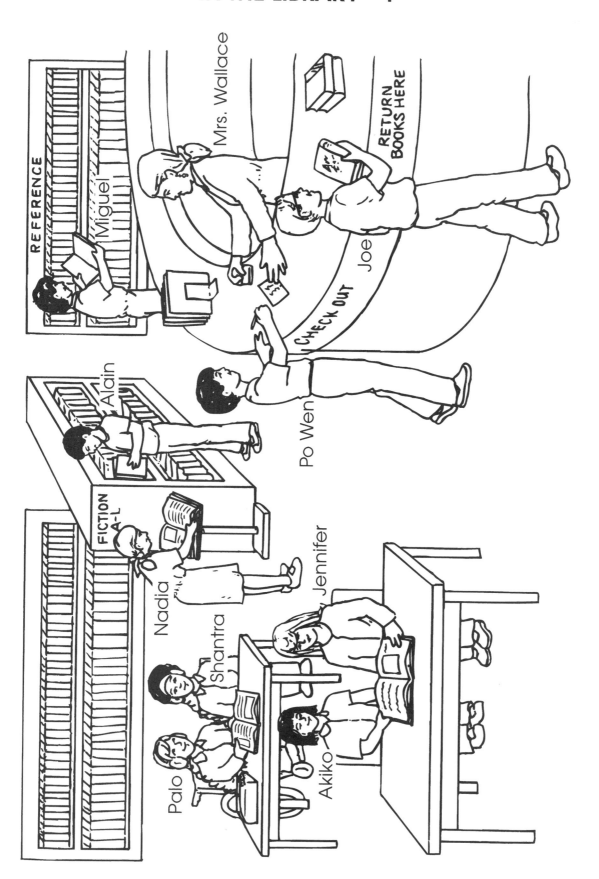

IN THE LIBRARY - 2

I. Look, listen, and read.

This is the library. The librarian's name is Mrs. Wallace. Mrs. Wallace is helping Po Wen. He is checking out a book. Joe is returning a book. Akiko and Jennifer are looking at a magazine. Palo and Shantra are listening to a story. They are using a tape recorder and headphones. Nadia is looking up a word in the dictionary. Alain is taking a book from the shelf. Miguel is using the encyclopedia.

II. YES or NO ?

1. The librarian's name is Mrs. Wallace. _____

2. Mrs. Wallace is reading a book. _____

3. Nadia is looking up a word in the dictionary. _____

4. Akiko and Jennifer are listening to a story. _____

5. Alain is checking out a book. _____

6. Po Wen is returning a book. _____

7. Miguel is looking at a magazine. _____

8. Palo and Shantra are using a tape recorder. _____

   See directions on page 10.

IN THE LIBRARY - 3

WORD BOX

shelf	checking out	returning	taking	dictionary
helping	headphones	librarian	magazine	encyclopedia

Listen, read, and write.

This is the library. The _____'s name is Mrs.
Wallace. Mrs. Wallace is _____ Po Wen. He is
_____ a book. Joe is _____
a book. Akiko and Jennifer are looking at a _____.
Palo and Shantra are listening to a story. They are using a tape
recorder and _____. Nadia is looking up a word
in the _____. Alain is _____
a book from the _____. Miguel is using the
_____.

IN THE LIBRARY - 4

Draw a picture for each sentence.

1. A girl is reading a magazine.

2. Two students are listening to a story.

3. A boy is looking up a word in the dictionary.

4. A girl is taking a book from the shelf.

5. The librarian is sitting at her desk.

6. A boy is using headphones.

 See directions on page 10.

IN THE LIBRARY - 5

ACROSS

2. Alain is _____ a book from the shelf.

4. Mrs. Wallace is the _____.

7.

11. Joe is _____ a book.

12.

13. Palo and Shantra are _____ to a story.

DOWN

1.

3. Akiko and Jennifer are looking at a _____.

5.

6.

8. Po Wen is _____ a book from the library.

9. Nadia is _____ a word in the dictionary.

10.

14.

See directions on page 10.

IN THE NURSE'S OFFICE - 1

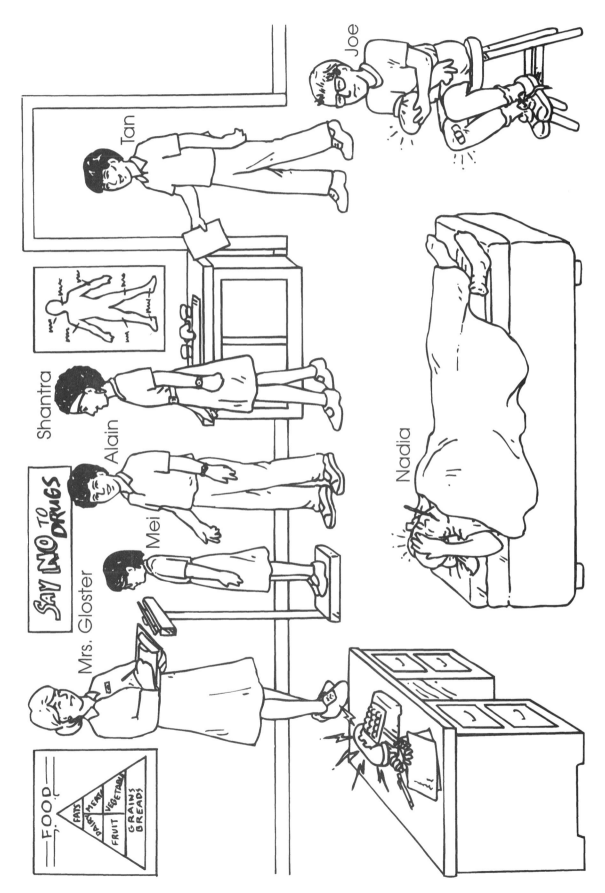

See directions on page 10.

IN THE NURSE'S OFFICE - 2

I. Look, listen, and read.

This is the nurse's office. The nurse's name is Ms. Gloster. Mei is on the scale. She is being weighed. Alain and Shantra are waiting for their turn. The telephone is ringing. Nadia is sick. She has a headache. She is lying down. She has a thermometer in her mouth. Joe hurt his elbow and his knee. He has an ice pack on his elbow. He has a bandaid on his knee. Tan is bringing a note to Ms. Gloster.

II. YES or NO ?

1. This is the gym class.   _____

2. Alain and Shantra are on the scale   _____

3. The nurse's name is Ms. Gloster.   _____

4. Alain is lying down.   _____

5. Joe has a bandaid on his knee.   _____

6. Tan has a headache.   _____

7. Nadia is bringing a note to Ms. Gloster.   _____

See directions on page 10.

IN THE NURSE'S OFFICE - 3

WORD BOX

bringing	waiting	sick	scale	nurse
ice pack	thermometer	hurt	bandaid	headache

Listen, read and write.

This is the _____'s office. The nurse's name is Ms. Gloster.

Mei is on the _____. She is getting weighed. Alain and

Shantra are _____ for their turn. The telephone is ringing.

Nadia is _____. She has a _____. She is lying

down. She has a _____ in her mouth. Joe_____ his

elbow and his knee. He has an _____ on his elbow. He

has a _____ on his knee. Tan is _____ a

note to Ms. Gloster.

                    See directions on page 10.

IN THE NURSE'S OFFICE - 4

Draw a picture for each sentence.

1. A nurse is weighing a girl.

2. The telephone is ringing.

3. A boy has an ice pack on his elbow.

4. A girl has a bandaid on her knee.

5. A girl is lying down.

6. A boy is bringing a note to the teacher.

See directions on page 10.

IN THE NURSE'S OFFICE - 5

Complete the crossword puzzle, using the picture clues below.

ACROSS

3.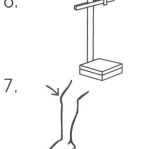

5.

6.

7.

8.

9

DOWN

1.

2.

3

4.

5.

See directions on page 10.

IN SCIENCE CLASS - 1

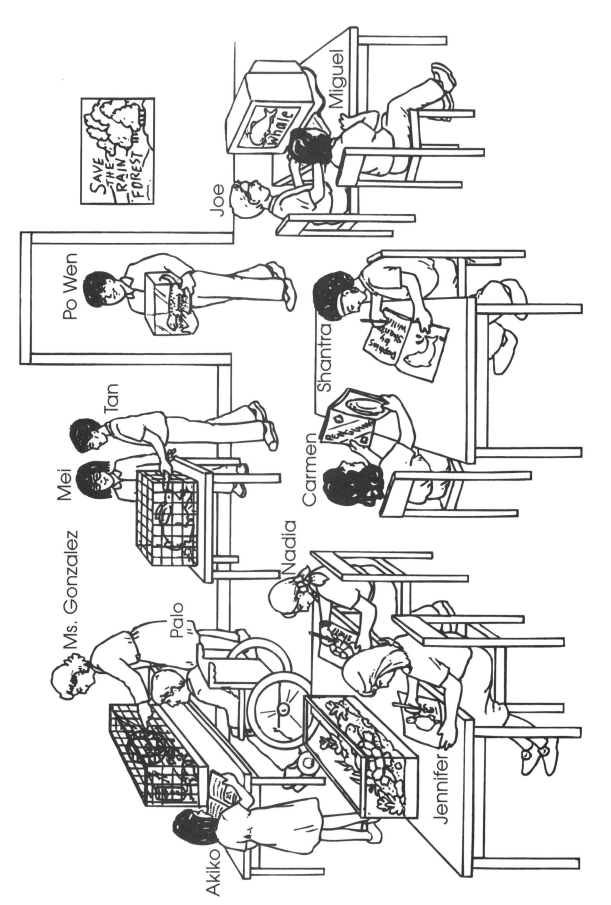

IN SCIENCE CLASS - 2

I. Look, listen, and read.

This is science class. The class is studying animals. The science teacher's name is Ms. Gonzalez. Palo and Akiko are observing white mice. Tan and Mei are feeding a rabbit. The rabbit is in the cage. Joe and Miguel are at the computer. They are studying whales. A turtle is in the terrarium. Jennifer and Nadia are drawing and labeling pictures of the turtle. Carmen is reading a book about penguins. Shantra is writing a report about dolphins. Po Wen is bringing his iguana to school.

II. Match.

1. Jennifer _____   A. are feeding a rabbit.

2. Po Wen _____   B. is writing a report about dolphins.

3. Tan and Mei _____   C. in a terrarium.

4. Shantra _____   D. are observing white mice.

5. The turtle is _____   E. is reading a book about penguins.

6. Ms. Gonzalez _____   F. is bringing his iguana to school.

7. The rabbit _____   G. is labeling a picture of a turtle.

8. Carmen _____   H. is in a cage.

9. Palo and Akiko _____   I. is the science teacher.

III. Copy the sentences on another sheet of paper.

          See directions on page 10.

Name _____   Date _____

IN SCIENCE CLASS - 3

WORD BOX

studying	iguana	observing	mice	report
penguins	labeling	whales	turtle	dolphins
rabbit	feeding	cage	terrarium	

Listen, read, and write.

This is science class. The class is_____ animals.

The science teacher's name is Ms. Gonzalez. Palo and Akiko are

_____ white_____. Tan and Mei are

_____ a rabbit. The rabbit is in a _____. Joe

and Miguel are at the computer. They are studying _____. A

_____ is in the _____. Jennifer and Nadia are

drawing and _____ pictures of the turtle. Carmen is

reading a book about _____. Shantra is writing a

_____ about _____. Po Wen is bringing his

_____ to class.

IN SCIENCE CLASS - 4

Draw a picture to go with each sentence.

1. A rabbit is in a cage.

2. A girl is feeding the rabbit.

3. A turtle is in a terrarium.

4. A boy is at a computer.

5. A girl is reading a book about penguins.

6. A boy is writing a report about dolphins.

 See directions on page 10.

IN SCIENCE CLASS - 5

Use the picture clues below to complete the crossword puzzle.

ACROSS

6.

8.

9.

10.

12.

13.

15.

DOWN

1.

2.

3.

4.

5.

7.

8.

11.

14.

IN THE COMPUTER ROOM - 1

See directions on page 10.

IN THE COMPUTER ROOM - 2

I. Look, listen, and read.

This is the computer room. The computer teacher's name is Mr. Kim. Mr. Kim is showing the class how to make a banner. Akiko is putting a   CD in the disk drive.   Jennifer is typing on a keyboard. The printer is printing Shantra's banner. Joe is watching. Miguel is teaching Carmen how to use the mouse. Alain and Mei are playing a computer game. They are looking at the computer screen. Tan's computer doesn't work.

II. YES or NO ?

1. Akiko and Jennifer are playing a computer game.   _____

2. The teacher's name is Mrs. Kim.   _____

3. Jennifer is typing on a keyboard.   _____

4. Mr. Kim is showing the class how to make a banner.   _____

5. Carmen is teaching Miguel to use the mouse.   _____

6. Mei is playing a computer game.   _____

7. Shantra is printing a banner.   _____

8. Joe is putting a CD in the disk drive.   _____

9. Tan's computer doesn't work.   _____

See directions on page 10.

IN THE COMPUTER ROOM - 3

WORD BOX

printing	mouse	keyboard	CD	screen
teaching	room	disk drive	banner	work

Listen, read, and write.

This is the computer_____. The computer teacher's

name is Mr. Kim. Mr. Kim is showing the class how to make a

_____. Akiko is putting a_____ in

the _____ _____. Jennifer is typing on the

_____. The printer is _____ Shantra's

banner. Joe is watching. Miguel is _____ Carmen how

to use the _____. Akiko and Mei are playing a computer

game. They are looking at the computer _____. Tan's

computer doesn't _____.

See directions on page 10.

IN THE COMPUTER ROOM - 4

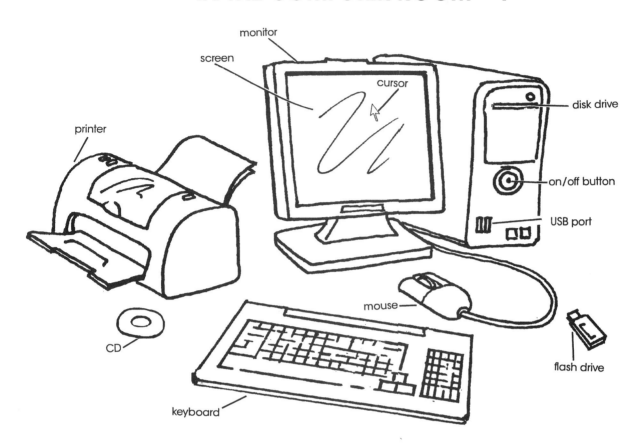

Fill in the correct words.

1 You type on the _____.

2. You put a _____ in the disk drive.

3. The mouse can move the _____ on the screen.

4. The _____ turns off the computer.

5. When you type on the keyboard, you see your work on the computer _____.

6. The screen is part of the _____.

IN THE COMPUTER ROOM - 5

I. Find and circle these words in the puzzle.

banner	computer	√ watching	disk drive	game
mouse	keyboard	printing	CD	play
printer	putting	show	teacher	screen
watching	looking	work	typing	showing

```
W A T C H I N G G M Z L K A L
O I Z C X B A N N E R G E E O
R Y I A U C R K V A F I Y S O
K B T B P R I N T I N G B C K
T E A C H E R Z F Z L C O R I
S S I G A M E C I Q P O A E N
X T Q T Y P I N G S U M R E G
I D I S K D R I V E T P D N U
G X T R W R J B O Q T U C L R
A R J M O U S E X V I T Q X F
O O H V P S H Z L Y N E M U K
S O H M P L A Y I N G R B K J
H M V M U U N S H O W I N G N
O R F L O P P C D I J K I H H
W L D M Q P R I N T E R F G B
```

See directions on page 10.

THE GRASSHOPPER AND THE ANTS - 1

I. Look, listen, and read.

KEY WORDS: Write these words in your language. Find the words in the story and underline them.

grasshopper	summer	winter	ants	plenty	warm
remember	saving	closed	play	food	work

The grasshopper loved to play. He did not like to work. One summer day he saw some ants. The ants were working.

"Why are you working?" asked the grasshopper. "It's summer. It's warm and there is plenty of food to eat."

"Yes, it is summer now," said the ants. "But winter will come soon. It is not easy to find food in the winter. We are making a warm home and saving food."

The grasshopper laughed at the ants. "Winter is a long time away," he said.

But winter came. The grasshopper was very cold. He had nothing to eat. He was very hungry.

Then he remembered the ants. He went to their home. "Ants, I am cold and hungry. Can you let me come in ? Can you give me some food ?" asked the grasshopper.

"No," said the ants. You played all summer. Now you can play all winter, too." The ants closed the door.

See directions on page 12.

THE GRASSHOPPER AND THE ANTS - 2

WORD BOX

loved	summer	winter	closed	easy	grasshopper
saving	plenty	laughed	nothing	work	remembered

Listen, read, and write.

The grasshopper _____ to play. He did not like to

_____. One _____ day he saw some

ants. The ants were working.

"Why are you working?" asked the grasshopper. "It's summer.

It's warm and there is _____ of food to eat."

"Yes, it is summer now," said the ants. "But _____ will

come soon. It is not _____ to find food in the winter. We

are making a warm home and _____ food."

The grasshopper _____ at the ants. "Winter is a

long time away," he said.

But winter came. The grasshopper was very cold. He had

_____ to eat. He was very hungry.

Then he _____ the ants. He went to their

home. "Ants, I am cold and hungry. Can you let me come in ? Can

you give me some food?" asked the _____.

"No." said the ants. You played all summer. Now you can play

all winter, too." The ants _____ the door.

        See directions on page 12.

THE GRASSHOPPER AND THE ANTS - 3

I. Match the opposite words.

1. go __F__   A. closed

2. summer_____   B. cold

3. yes_____   C. work

4. night _____   D. day

5. play _____   E. no

6. hot _____   F. come

7. opened _____   G. winter

II. Choose the best answer. Fill in the square.

1. Who did not like to work ?   ■ the grasshopper □ the ants

2. Who was saving food ?   □ the grasshopper □ the ants

3. Who thought winter was a long time away ?
                              □ the grasshopper □ the ants

4. Who was not hungry in the winter ?
                              □ the grasshopper □ the ants

5. Who asked for food ?   □ the grasshopper □ the ants

6. Who said, "No ?"   □ the grasshopper □ the ants

7. Who closed the door ?   □ the grasshopper □ the ants

See directions on page 12.

THE GRASSHOPPER AND THE ANTS - 4

Find and circle these words in the puzzle below.

√away	closed	cold	laughed	give
easy	food	home	grasshopper	no
play	some	summer	remember	warm
soon	winter	like	hungry	ant

```
G Q G U E K E W Y J C B B Y
L M L Y W A A G T E O T T U
I D S O O N S Y S P L A Y I
K Q W A R M Y Y E H D S B Q
E D J L K M S M X O Q M E G
G R A S S H O P P E R M Y I
A E D U T H A N T E O T Z V
R E M E M B E R K C N E D E
E C L O S E D N B E X H N N
H L S U M M E R L D U U O R
F O O D I W H P M A T N X S
N N H H Y W I N T E R G M O
Q G L A U G H E D B U R D M
F C D E U V E A W A Y Y T E
```

See directions on page 12.

THE GRASSHOPPER AND THE ANTS - 5

Show what the grasshopper and the ants are saying.

See directions on page 12.

THE HUNGRY FOX - 1

Look, listen, and read.

KEY WORDS: Write these words in your language. Find the
words in the story and underline them.

shepherd	place	hole	dinner
stuck	inside	heard	
squeezed		nobody	

One day a shepherd put a bag of food in a hole in a tree. "This
is a good place to hide my dinner," said the shepherd.

A hungry fox was watching the shepherd. He said, "I am so
hungry. What a good dinner that is!"

The fox waited. Finally, the shepherd went off to watch his sheep.
The fox squeezed into the hole in the tree. He was happy to eat such
good food, so he ate, and he ate.

The fox ate so much that he was too fat to get out of the tree.
"Help!" he cried, but nobody heard him. He was stuck inside the hole.

    See directions on page 12.

THE HUNGRY FOX - 2

WORD BOX

shepherd	place	what	finally	stuck	fat
squeezed	hole	much	dinner	nobody	hungry

I. Listen, read, and write.

One day a _____ put a bag of food in a _____ in a tree. "This is a good _____ to hide my _____," said the shepherd.

A _____ fox was watching the shepherd. He said, "I am so hungry. _____ a good dinner that is!"

The fox waited. _____, the shepherd went to watch his sheep. The fox _____ into the hole in the tree. He was happy to eat such good food, so he ate and he ate and he ate.

The fox ate so _____ that he was too _____ to get out of the tree. "Help!" he cried, but _____ heard him. He was _____ inside the hole!

See directions on page 12.

THE HUNGRY FOX - 3

I. Match each verb with its correct past form.

1. hear __F__   A. ate

2. go _____   B. was

3. find _____   C. went

4. say _____   D. said

5. eat _____   E. found

6. is _____   F. heard

II. YES or NO?

1. A fox found some food in a house.   __No__

2. A sheep put a bag of food in a hole in a tree.   _____

3. "This is a good place to hide my sheep," said the shepherd.   _____

4. A hungry fox was watching the shepherd.   _____

5. "What a good dinner that is!" said the fox.   _____

6. The fox squeezed into the hole in the tree.   _____

7. The fox ate and ate.   _____

8. "Help!" cried the sheep.   _____

          See directions on page 12

Name _____ Date _____

THE HUNGRY FOX - 4

Complete the puzzle.

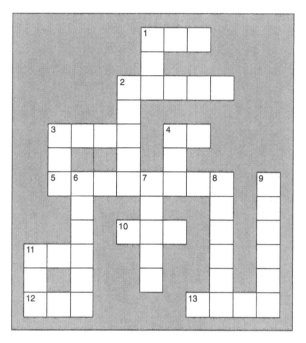

ACROSS

1.

2. He was _____ inside!

3.

4. The fox said, "I _____ so hungry."

5.

10. A hungry fox _____ watching the shepherd.

11.

12. Opposite of night

13.

DOWN

1. The fox was too _____ to get out of the hole.

2.

3. The shepherd went to watch _____ sheep.

4. The fox _____ so much that he was too fat.

6. The fox said, "I am so _____."

7. "Help!" he cried, but nobody _____ the fox.

8. "What a good _____ that is!" said the fox.

9. The fox was stuck _____ the hole.

11. Opposite of good.

See directions on page 12.   © 1995 by Elizabeth Claire and Barbara J. Haynes

THE HUNGRY FOX - 5

Write what the shepherd and the fox are thinking or saying.

See directions on page 12.

THE BOY AND THE WOLF - 1

KEY WORDS: Write these words in your language. Find the words in the story and underline them.

sheep	wolf	again	think/thought
job	watching	hungry	boring
go/went	village	fool/fooled	come/came

Look, listen, and read.

A boy was watching sheep. "This job is boring. I want to have fun," he thought. "Help! Help! A wolf!" he cried.

The people from the village ran to help him. "Where is the wolf?" they asked.

"Ha, ha! I fooled you," said the boy. "There is no wolf." The people went back to the village.

The next day, the boy again cried, "Help! Help! A wolf!"

Again the people came. And again there was no wolf.

"Ha, ha! I fooled you!" said the boy again.

Later, a hungry wolf came. He started to eat the sheep.

"Help! Help! A wolf!" cried the boy.

But the people did not want to be fooled again. Nobody came to help the boy. So the wolf ate all the sheep.

See directions on page 12.

THE BOY AND THE WOLF - 2

WORD BOX

watching	boring	nobody	started	want	again
thought	Where	fooled	people	hungry	all

Listen, read, and write.

A boy was _____ sheep. "This job is _____. I want

to have fun," he _____. "Help! Help! A wolf!" he cried.

The _____ from the village ran to help him.

_____ is the wolf?" they asked.

"Ha, ha! I _____ you." said the boy.

"There is no wolf."   The people went back to the village.

The next day, the boy _____ cried, "Help! Help! A

Wolf!" Again the people came. And again there was no wolf.

"Ha, ha! I fooled you," said the boy again. Later, a

_____ wolf came. He _____ to eat the

sheep. "Help! Help! A wolf!"cried the boy.

But the people did not _____ to be fooled again.

_____ came to help the boy. So the wolf ate _____

the sheep.

    See directions on page 12.

THE BOY AND THE WOLF - 3

I. Put the sentences in the correct order. Use the story text to help you.

_____ a. The boy cried, "Help! Help! A wolf !"

_____ b. The wolf ate all the sheep.

_____ c. The people from the village asked, "Where is the wolf ?"

__1__ d. A boy was watching sheep.

_____ e. Again, the boy cried, "Help! Help! A wolf!"

_____ f. Nobody came to help the boy.

_____ g. The boy said, "Ha, ha! I fooled you."

_____ h. The people from the village ran to help him.

II. Copy the sentences in the correct story order.

III. YES or NO ?

1. A girl was watching sheep.   _____

2. The job was boring.   _____

3. The boy cried, "Help! Help! A sheep!"   _____

4. The boy fooled the people in the village.   _____

5. Later, a hungry fox ate the sheep.   _____

6. The people came and stopped the wolf.   _____

7. The wolf ate all the people.   _____

See directions on page 12.

THE BOY AND THE WOLF - 4

I. Find and circle these words in the puzzle below.

again	came	hungry	started	all
come	job	village	fooled	ate
later	back	fun	watching	help
people	boring	√sheep	where	wolf

```
F O O L E D K A L L K P Z
L F W A H A B A C K J L R
W S A T A S T A R T E D W
H H T E V I L L A G E G O
E E C R L H J C O M E A L
R E H Z A E I R Q G N W F
E P I P T L H U N G R Y B
A L N E E P Q I B Y M B Z
G L G O W N J Y O J H V O
A O K P C A M E R A S T F
I H B L J S F E I N O M V
N C D E O N U B N N V O V
O Y U V B Q N W G D T K M
```

See directions on page 12.

THE BOY AND THE WOLF - 5

Show what the boy and the people are saying or thinking.

© 1995 by Elizabeth Claire and Barbara J. Haynes

THE FOX AND THE BOAR - 1

I. Look, listen and read.

KEY WORDS: Write these words in your language. Find the words in the story and underline them.

sharpening	tusks	trunk	boar	answer
rubbing	against	safe	danger	woods
terrible	hear/heard	begin/began		wild

An old fox was walking in the woods. He heard a lot of noise. "What's that terrible noise ?" said the old fox. He saw a wild boar rubbing his tusks against a tree trunk. "What are you doing?" asked the fox.

"I am sharpening my tusks," answered the wild boar.

"Why are you doing that now?" the fox asked. "You are safe here."

"Silly old fox," the boar said. "I must make my tusks sharp now. If I wait until there is danger, there will not be time."And he began to rub his tusks again.

 See directions on page 12.

THE FOX AND THE BOAR - 2

WORD BOX

danger	began	noise	terrible	tusks
safe	silly	woods	rubbing	sharpening

Listen, read, and write.

An old fox was walking in the _____. He heard a lot of

_____. "What's that _____ noise ?" said the old

fox. He saw a wild boar _____ his _____

against a tree trunk. "What are you doing?" asked the fox.

"I am _____ my tusks," answered the

boar.

"Why are you doing that now ?" the fox asked. "You are

_____ here."

"_____ old fox," the boar said. "I must make my

tusks sharp now. If I wait until there is _____, there will not

be time." And he _____ to rub his tusks again.

THE FOX AND THE BOAR - 3

I. Find and circle these words in the puzzle.

trunk	safe	tusks	began	noise	heard
time	old	boar	danger	sharp	wild
fox	woods	silly	walk	terrible	

```
T  R  S  A  O  L  D  F  E  T  U  X
N  O  S  L  W  T  A  N  O  I  S  E
B  B  O  T  R  U  N  K  A  R  H  S
W  E  L  I  T  S  G  E  G  K  A  I
F  G  O  M  X  K  E  W  D  S  R  L
S  A  F  E  M  S  R  D  I  N  P  W
G  N  T  B  S  O  A  T  F  O  L  I
T  E  R  R  I  B  L  E  G  S  A  L
F  W  O  T  L  A  K  H  E  A  R  D
O  A  W  A  L  K  W  O  O  D  S  G
X  N  N  M  Y  E  F  B  O  A  R  L
```

II. Put an X in the correct squares.

1. The wild boar was ☐ quiet.
   ☐ noisy.

2. The wild boar ☐ was sleeping.
   ☐ was rubbing his tusks.

4. The wild boar ☐ wanted sharp tusks.
   ☐ wanted a good dinner.

5. The old fox said, ☐ "You are safe here."
   ☐ "You are a silly animal."

6. The wild boar said, ☐ "Silly old fox."
   ☐ "Thank you for helping me."

 See directions on page 12.

Name _____ Date _____

THE FOX AND THE BOAR - 4

Complete the puzzle, using the clues below.

Across

3. Part of a tree.

5. Short for "what is."

7. When it is not safe, there is _____.

9. Opposite of unsafe.

10. "What's that _____ noise?"

11. "_____ old fox," the boar said.

12. Opposite of coming.

Down

1. Opposite of stopped.

2. Opposite of aren't.

4. Opposite of quiet is _____.

5. Another word for forest

6. "I am _____ my tusks."

8. Opposite of answered.

13. "Silly _____ fox"

14. Opposite of later.

See directions on page 12.

THE FOX AND THE BOAR - 5

Show what the fox and the wild boar are saying.

See directions on page 12.

Name _____   Date _____

SCRAMBLED SENTENCES - 1

Write these words in the correct order to make good sentences.

1. boy A sheep. watching was

_____

2. sheep. The ate all wolf the

_____

3. people The back work. to went

_____

4. job This boring. is

_____

5. came. wolf hungry a Later

_____

6. the sheep. started He to eat

_____

7. came Nobody boy. the help to

_____

See directions on page 12.

SCRAMBLED SENTENCES - 2

Write these words in the correct order to make good sentences.

1. noise? terrible that What's

_____

2. must I tusks my now. sharp make

_____

3. again. to rub He his tusks began

_____

4. dinner is! that good What a

_____

5. stuck was tree. inside He the

_____

6. was watching A the shepherd. fox hungry

_____

7. dinner. This my hide place to a is good

_____

8. like not The work. to grasshopper did

_____

See directions on page 12.

Name _____   Date _____

FARM OR ZOO ?

Where can you find these animals? Paste the pictures in the correct column.

 FARM | ZOO

© 1995 by Elizabeth Claire and Barbara J. Haynes

WHICH ANIMALS BELONG TOGETHER?

Look at the animals in each row. Cut out the pictures below and paste them in the correct row.

cow	horse	pig	
grasshopper	spider	bee	
octopus	seahorse	shark	
elephant	zebra	giraffe	

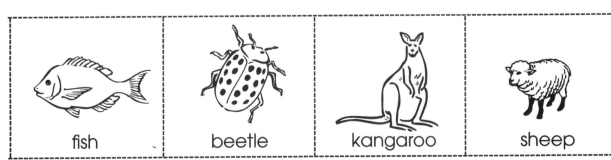

fish	beetle	kangaroo	sheep

See directions on page 13.

HOW DO ANIMALS MOVE?

**Look at the pictures of the animals below. How do they move?
Cut out each picture and paste it in the correct column.**

FLY	HOP/JUMP	WALK/RUN	SWIM

grasshopper | whale | frog | bee | rabbit | dolphin

bear | seal | bat | moose | zebra | owl

FUR, FEATHERS OR SCALES?

Cut out the pictures. Paste them in the correct column.

FUR (HAIR)	FEATHERS	SCALES

See directions on page 13.

ANIMALS AND THEIR BABIES

Draw a line from the name of each animal to the picture of its baby:

1. cow

2. horse

3. deer

4. kangaroo

5. sheep

6. lion

7 goose

8. goat

a. cub

b. joey

c. calf

d. fawn

e. gosling

f. kid

g. foal

h. lamb

See directions on page 13.

WHAT DO ANIMALS EAT ?

Which animals eat plants? Which animals eat other animals? Cut out the pictures and paste them in the correct column.

PLANTS	ANIMALS

seal	deer	tiger	polar bear	hippopotamus	rabbit
owl	crocodile	eagle	elephant	zebra	giraffe

　　　　See directions on page 13.

WHAT'S THE TEMPERATURE? - 1

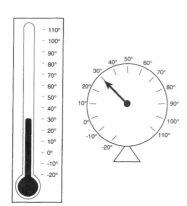
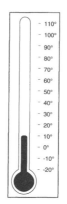

1. These are thermometers. A thermometer measures the temperature.

It's 10°.

2. Temperature is measured in degrees. The symbol for degrees is °. 10° = 10 degrees.

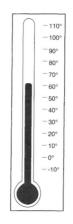

3. There are two kinds of scales. The Celsius (C) scale and the Fahrenheit (F) scale.

Write these temperatures in words.

1. 20° __twenty degrees Fahrenheit_____

2. 80° _____

3. 15° _____

WHAT'S THE TEMPERATURE?-2

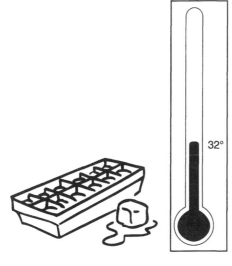

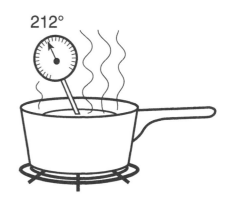

1. It is 32° Fahrenheit. Water freezes at this temperature.

2. It is 212° Fahrenheit. Water boils at this temperature.

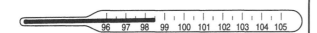

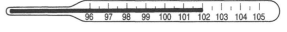

3. Normal body temperature is 98.6° F

4. Tan's temperature is 102°. He has a fever.

Write the temperatures that these thermometers show.

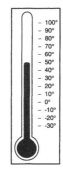
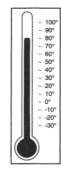
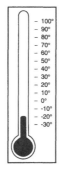
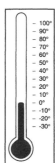

a._____   b._____   c._____   d._____

See directions on page 14.

Name _____ Date _____

WHAT'S THE TEMPERATURE?-3

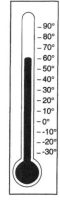

1. These are _____

2. They measure _____

3. There are two different scales: _____ and
   _____

4. The temperature is _____ Fahrenheit.

5. Water freezes at _____ Fahrenheit.

6. Water boils at _____ Fahrenheit.

7. Normal body temperature is _____ Fahrenheit.

8. A temperature of 103° is a _____.

Fahrenheit	Celsius	thermometers
212°	fever	32°
temperature	98.6°	

9. The temperature in the room now is _____ F.

10. The temperature outside now is _____ F.

WHAT'S THE TEMPERATURE-4

1. It is a hot day.
   How hot is it?
   It is ____ degrees Fahrenheit.
   (_____° F.)

2. It is a cold day.
   How cold is it? It is
   ____ degrees Fahrenheit
   (_____° F.)

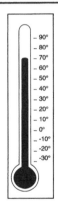

3. It is a warm day. It is _____ ° F.

4. It is a cool day. It is _____° F.

5. Akiko is well. Her temperature
   is _____° F.

6. Joe has a fever. How high is
   his fever? His temperature is
   _____ ° F.

1. What is the temperature outside now? _____

2. What is the temperature inside? _____

3. What is your temperature today? _____

See directions on page 14.

WHAT'S THE WEATHER? - 1

the sun

clouds

1. The sun is shining.
   It's a sunny day.

2. It's a cloudy day.

3. It's partly cloudy.

fog

rain

4. It's foggy.

5. It's raining.

6. It's pouring.

snow

sleet

hailstones

7. It's snowing.

8. It's sleeting.

9. It's hailing.

See directions on page 15.

WHAT'S THE WEATHER? - 2

wind

storm clouds

lightning   thunder

10. It's windy.   11. It's a thunderstorm.

12. It's a hurricane.   13. It's a tornado.   14. It's a blizzard.

smog

15. It's smoggy.   16. It's flooding.   17. It's a drought.

flood

     See directions on page 15.

TODAY'S WEATHER

1. Today, it is   ☐ hot   and   ☐ sunny.
    ☐ warm   ☐ cloudy.
    ☐ cool   ☐ partly cloudy.
    ☐ cold   ☐ foggy.

2. ☐ It's windy.
   ☐ It isn't windy.

3. ☐ It's raining.
   ☐ It isn't raining.

4. ☐ It's snowing.
   ☐ It isn't snowing.

5. At _____ (time) the temperature was _____ ° F.

Copy the sentences about today's weather.

_____

_____

_____

_____

_____

_____

YESTERDAY'S WEATHER

1. Yesterday, it was   ☐ hot   and   ☐ sunny.
   ☐ warm   ☐ cloudy.
   ☐ cool   ☐ partly cloudy.
   ☐ cold   ☐ foggy.

2. ☐ It was windy.
   ☐ It wasn't windy.

3. ☐ It rained.
   ☐ It didn't rain.

4. ☐ It snowed.
   ☐ It didn't snow.

5. At _____ (time) the temperature was _____ ° F.

Copy the sentences about yesterday's weather.

_____

_____

_____

_____

_____

_____

     See directions on page 15.

Name _____   Date _____

MY WEATHER FORECAST

1. Tomorrow, (date) _____ _____, it will be
   - ☐ hot   and   ☐ sunny.
   - ☐ warm   ☐ cloudy.
   - ☐ cool   ☐ partly cloudy.
   - ☐ cold   ☐ foggy.

2. ☐ It will be windy.
   ☐ It will not be windy.

3. ☐ It will rain.
   ☐ It won't rain.

4. ☐ It will snow.
   ☐ It won't snow.

5. At _____ (time) the temperature
   will be _____ °.   ?

Copy your weather forecast.

_____

_____

_____

_____

_____

_____

Check the weather the next day. Compare it to your forecast. Make a new forecast. Check your weather forecasts for two weeks.

See directions on page 15.

KEEP A WEATHER CALENDAR

1. **Keep a weather calendar for the next two weeks. Use these symbols.**

| sunny | cloudy | partly cloudy | rain | snow | storm | wind |

2. **Look at a thermometer each day. Make a mark on the chart to show the day's temperature. Draw a line to make a graph of the temperature for two weeks.**

Sample:

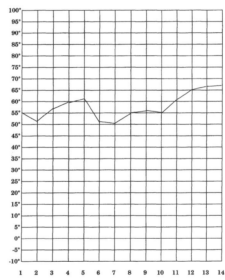

3. **When the calendar is finished, complete these sentences.**

a. _____ days were sunny.

b. _____ days were cloudy.

c. It rained on _____ days.

d. It snowed on _____ days.

e. The coldest temperature was _____.

f. The hottest temperature was _____.

    See directions on page 15.

Name _____ Date _____

MY WEATHER CALENDAR

First Week   Second Week

Sunday

Monday

Tuesday

Wednesday

Thursday

Friday

Saturday

See directions on page 15.

TEMPERATURE CHART

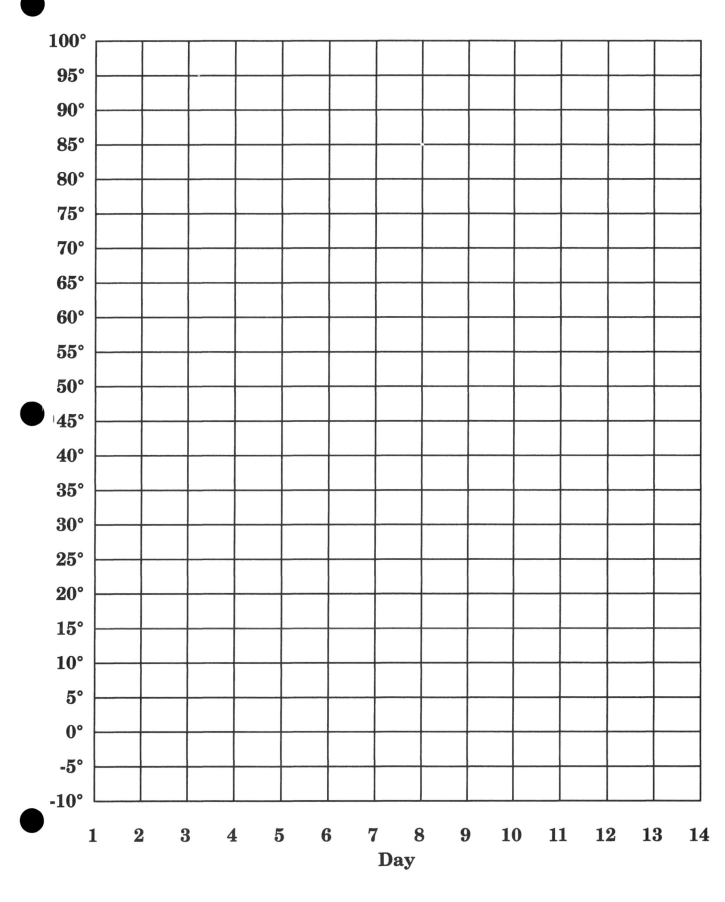

See directions on page 16.

THE PARTS OF A PLANT - 1

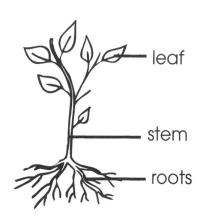

1. This is a plant. A plant has roots, a stem, and leaves.

2. Some plants have flowers. They are called flowering plants.

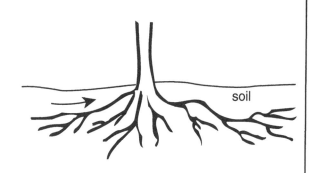

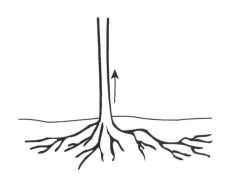

3. The roots keep the plant in the soil. They take water and minerals from the soil.

4. The stem holds the plant up. It moves minerals and water from the roots to the leaves.

5. Food for the plant is made in the leaves. This is called photosynthesis.

6. Seeds are made in the flowers. The seeds will grow into new plants.

PARTS OF A PLANT - 2

WORD BOX

plants	roots	minerals	seeds
flowers	leaves	flowering plants	
stem	soil	photosynthesis	

I. Write the correct word.

1. A plant has _____, a stem , and leaves.

2. Some plants have _____. They are called

   _____.

3. The roots keep the plant in the _____. They take

   water and _____ from the soil.

4. The _____ holds the plant up. It moves water and

   minerals from roots to the_____.

5. Food for the plant is made in the leaves. This is called

   _____.

6. _____ are made in the flowers. The seeds will grow

   into new _____.

          See directions on page 16.

Name _____ Date _____

THE PARTS OF A PLANT - 3

I. YES or NO?

1. The stem keeps the plant in the soil.   **No**

2. Food for the plant is made in the stem.   _____

3. The roots move water and minerals to the leaves.   _____

4. Some plants have flowers.   _____

5. Roots take water and minerals from the ground.   _____

6. Seeds are made in the stem.   _____

7. The stem holds the plant up.   _____

8. Seeds grow into new plants.   _____

II. Match.

1. flowering plant ___   a. Moves water and minerals from the roots to the leaves.

2. roots ___   b. Seeds are made in this part.

3. stem ___   c. Food for the plant is made here.

4. leaves ___   d. This part takes water and minerals from the soil.

5. flowers ___   e. Will grow into new plants.

6. seeds ___   f. A plant with flowers.

See directions on page 16.

HOW FLOWERS MAKE SEEDS - 1

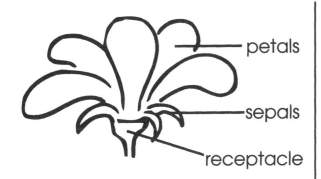

petals

sepals

receptacle

7. The outside part of a flower has petals, sepals and a receptacle.

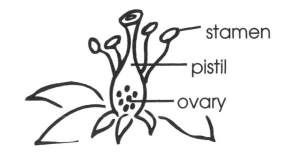

stamen

pistil

ovary

8. The inside part has the pistil and the stamen. The ovary is inside the pistil.

pollen _____

9. The stamen has pollen. Pollen falls into the pistil. This is called fertilization.

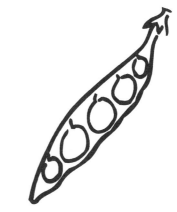

10. The ovary grows into a fruit that holds seeds. Seeds become new plants.

apple   pear   cherries   pepper   tomato   peas

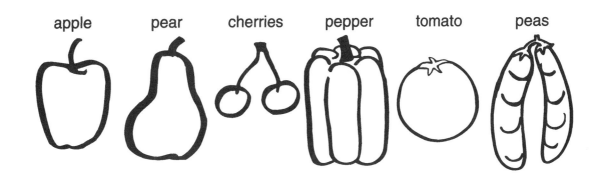

11. We eat many of the fruits of flowering plants. Some vegetables are really fruits because they hold seeds.

See directions on page 16.

Name _____ Date _____

HOW FLOWERS MAKE SEEDS - 2

WORD BOX

vegetables	stamen	pollen	pistil	fruits
seeds	hold	ovary	falls	fertilization

I. Write the correct word.

1. The inside part of the flower has the _____ and the

   _____.

2. The stamen has _____. Pollen _____ into

   the pistil. This is called_____.

3. The _____ grows into a fruit that holds

   _____. The seeds become new

   plants.

4. We eat many of the _____ of flowering plants.

   Some _____ are really fruits because they

   _____ seeds.

HOW FLOWERS MAKE SEEDS - 3

I. YES or NO?

1. Fertilization is when pollen falls into the pistil. _____

2. The ovary grows into a fruit that holds leaves. _____

3. We eat the pollen of many flowering plants. _____

4. Some vegetables are really fruits because they hold seeds. _____

II. Match.

1. pistil and stamen _____   A. contains seeds

2. seeds _____   B. inside parts of a flower

3. fruit _____   C. falls into the pistil

4. ovary _____   D. contains pollen

5. pollen _____   E. grows into a fruit

6. stamen _____   F. are kept in the fruit of
                                        flowering plants

III. Which of these foods are fruits of a flowering plant? Use your dictionary if you don't know.

1. carrot _____	5. broccoli _____	9. peas _____
2. asparagus _____	6. cherry _____	10. green beans _____
3. apple __√__	7. potato _____	11. strawberry _____
4. tomato _____	8. orange _____	12. lettuce _____

          See directions on page 16.

PLANT QUIZ

Match.

1. roots _____   A. plants that have flowers

2. stem _____   B. inside parts of a flower

3. leaves _____   C. take water and minerals to
                                     leaves

4. flowers _____   D. falls into the pistil

5. seeds _____   E. keeps the plant in the soil

6. fruit _____   F. outside part of the flower

7. flowering plant _____   G. when pollen falls into the pistil

8. pistil and stamen _____   H. food for the plant is made
                                     here

9. soil _____   I. become new plants

10. petals, sepals and   J. part of the plant that makes
    receptacle _____   seeds

11. fertilization _____   K. part of the plant where seeds
                                     are kept

12. pollen _____   L. ground, earth

Name _____ Date _____

LABEL THE PARTS OF A PLANT

7

1 **stamen**

8

9

2

3

4

5

6

10

11

12

13

Label the parts of a flowering plant.

seed   leaf   flower   pistil

roots   sepals   stem   fruit

ovary   petals   √ stamen   pollen

receptacle

See directions on page 16.

Name _____ Date _____

WRITE THE NUMBERS

a. seven __7__   four _____   five _____   two _____

b. ten _____   nine _____   three _____   eight _____

c. zero _____   six _____   eleven _____   thirteen _____

d. fifteen _____   eighteen _____   twenty _____   twelve _____

e. thirty _____   fourteen _____   forty _____   fifty _____

f. twenty-five _____   thirty-seven _____   forty-eight _____

g. eighty-seven _____   ninety-three _____   fifty-two _____

h. one hundred _____   two hundred ten _____

i. four hundred twelve _____   nine hundred thirteen _____

j. eight hundred twenty-four _____

k. three hundred fifty-nine _____

l. one thousand _____   four thousand seven hundred _____

m. five thousand eight hundred twenty-four _____

n. eight thousand four hundred ninety-three _____

o. two thousand six hundred twenty-nine _____

See directions on page 17.   © 1995 by Elizabeth Claire and Barbara J. Haynes

DRAW THE HANDS ON THE CLOCKS

It's two o'clock.

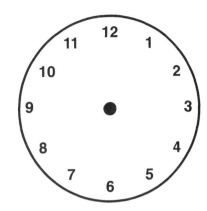

It's two ten.

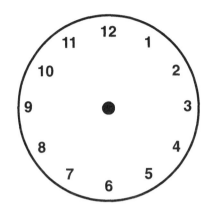

It's two fifteen.

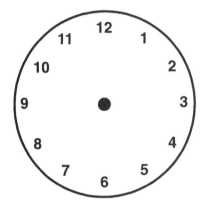

It's two twenty-five.

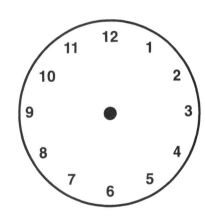

It's two thirty.

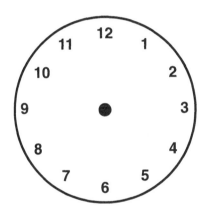

It's two forty.

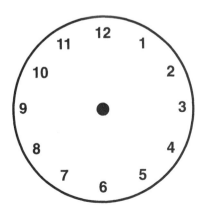

It's two forty-five.

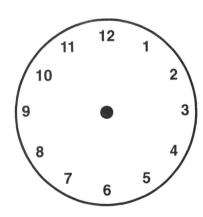

It's two fifty-nine.

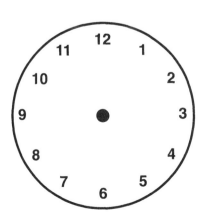

It's three o'clock.

See directions on page 17.

WHAT TIME IS IT?

A.
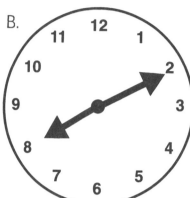

It's eight o'clock.

B.

C.
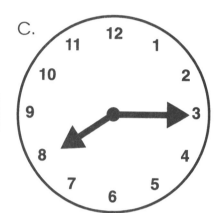

D.

E.
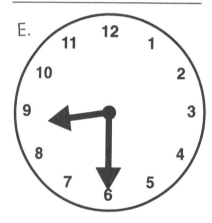

F.
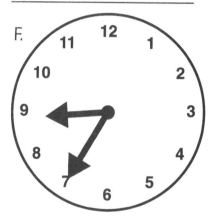

G.

H.

I.

MATH SYMBOLS

$+$ plus	$-$ minus	$\times$ times (multiplied by)	$\div$ divided by
$=$ equals	$\neq$ is not equal to	$>$ is greater than	$<$ is less than
$\sqrt{}$ square root	¢ cents	$ dollars	% percent	$\frac{^{2}}{}$ square

Use numbers and symbols to write these sentences.

1. Four plus seven equals eleven. __4 + 7 = 11__

2. Six minus two equals four. _____

3. Five times ten equals fifty. _____

4. Twelve divided by four equals three. _____

5. Eight is greater than seven. _____

6. Nine is less than eleven. _____

7. twenty five cents _____

8. six dollars _____

9. one hundred percent _____

10. Five square equals twenty-five. _____

11. The square root of nine is three. _____

  See directions on page 18.

READ AND WRITE MATH SYMBOLS

Write these math statements in words.

1. a. 6 + 1 = 7.   b. 8 - 3 = 5   c. 4 x 6 = 24

2. a. 10 - 2 = 5   b. $3)\overline{12}$ with 4 above   c. 8 > 7

3. a. 3 < 4   b. 10%   c. 20¢

4. a. $3.45   b. $\sqrt{16}$ c. 3^2

1 a. __Six plus one equals seven.__ _____

 b. _____

 c. _____

2 a. _____

 b. _____

 c. _____

3 a. _____

 b. _____

 c. _____

4 a. _____

 b. _____

 c. _____

THE MULTIPLICATION TABLE

Write the missing numbers.

×	0	1	2	3	4	5	6	7	8	9	10
0	0	0	___	0	0	0	0	0	___	0	0
1	0	1	2	3	4	___	6	7	8	9	10
2	___	2	4	6	___	10	12	___	16	18	___
3	0	___	6	9	12	15	___	21	24	___	30
4	0	4	8	___	16	20	24	___	32	___	40
5	0	5	___	15	___	25	___	35	40	45	___
6	0	___	12	18	24	30	___	42	___	56	60
7	0	7	14	___	28	35	42	49	___	63	70
8	0	___	16	24	32	___	48	56	64	___	80
9	0	9	___	27	___	45	54	___	72	81	90
10	___	10	20	30	40	50	___	70	80	90	___

1. Eight times zero is __zero_____.

2. One times five is _____.

3. Two times four is _____.

4. Three times one is _____.

5. Four times three is _____.

6. _____ times two is ten.

7. _____ _____ _____ _____ _____.

  See directions on page 18.

U.S. COINS AND BILLS

			heads	tails

penny   (one cent)   (1¢)

nickel   (five cents)   (5¢)

dime   (ten cents)   (10¢)

quarter   (twenty-five cents)   (25¢)

half-dollar   (fifty cents)   (50¢)

silver dollar (one hundred cents) ($1)

dollar bill   (one hundred cents) ($1)

© 1995 by Elizabeth Claire and Barbara J. Haynes

HOW MUCH IS IT?

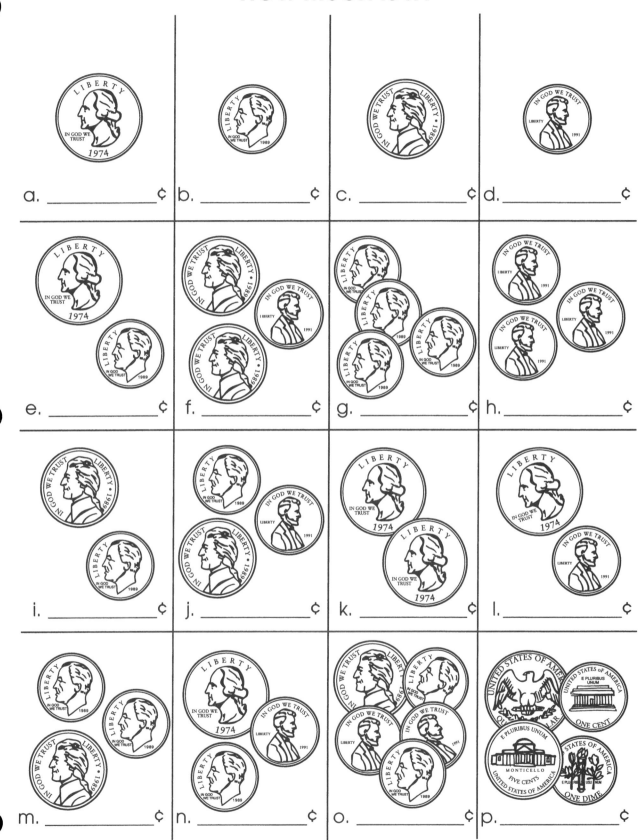

a. _____ ¢

b. _____ ¢

c. _____ ¢

d. _____ ¢

e. _____ ¢

f. _____ ¢

g. _____ ¢

h. _____ ¢

i. _____ ¢

j. _____ ¢

k. _____ ¢

l. _____ ¢

m. _____ ¢

n. _____ ¢

o. _____ ¢

p. _____ ¢

See directions on page 18.

READ AND WRITE ABOUT MONEY

$.25
25¢

a. Twenty five cents
    A quarter

$1.25

b. One dollar and twenty-five
    cents.
    A dollar twenty-five.
    One twenty-five.
    A dollar and a quarter.

$29.95

c. Twenty-nine dollars and
    ninety-five cents.
    Twenty-nine ninety-five.

$.75

d. _____

    _____

$1.75

e. _____

    _____

    _____

$28.85

f. _____

    _____

    _____

$67.01

g. _____

    _____

    _____

$44.29

h. _____

    _____

    _____

Name _____ Date _____ R85

SOLVE WORD PROBLEMS - 1

a.

Joe has six dollars.
Jennifer has four dollars. How
much money do they have
in all?

_____

b.

Carmen is carrying ten
books. Miguel is carrying
one book. How many books
are they carrying altogether?

_____

c.

Akiko is holding thirty balloons.
Nadia is holding forty balloons.
Palo is holding ninety balloons.
What is the total number of
balloons?

_____

d.

Jennifer went to the
movies. She spent five
dollars to get in, two
dollars on popcorn and
one dollar for peanuts.
How much did she spend
altogether?

_____

See directions on page 18.

SOLVE WORD PROBLEMS-2

a.

Tan has eight dollars. Mei has three dollars. How much more money does Tan have than Mei?

_____

b.

Palo had eleven dollars. He spent five dollars. How much money did he have left?

_____

c.

There were nine cookies on the plate. Shantra ate four cookies. How many cookies were left?

_____

d.

Akiko has twelve friends. She wants to make a gift for each one. She has already made seven. How many more must she make?

_____

SOLVE WORD PROBLEMS-3

a.

Po Wen wants to buy three apples. The apples are twenty cents each. How much money does he need?

_____

b.

Tan, Miguel, and Joe went to the movies. Each ticket cost four dollars. How much did they have to pay altogether?

_____

c.

Miguel ran five miles a day for six days. How many miles did he run altogether?

_____

d.

Jennifer, Palo, Shantra, and Akiko each have two boxes of cereal. How many boxes do they have altogether?

_____

     See directions on page 18.

SOLVE WORD PROBLEMS-4

a.

Jennifer bought six lemons.
She paid sixty cents. How much
did each lemon cost?

_____

b.

Eight students went in two
taxis. How many students
were in each taxi?

_____

c.

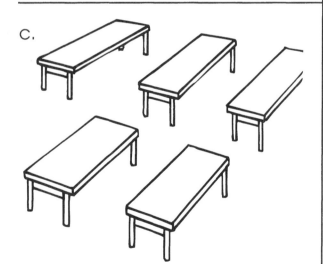

There are five tables in
the classroom. Twenty
students are in the class.
How many students sit at
each table?

_____

d.

Jennifer baked eighteen
cookies for Tan, Miguel,
and Po Wen. How many
cookies can each boy
have?

_____

See directions on page 18.   © 1995 by Elizabeth Claire and Barbara J. Haynes

READ THE NUMBERS: ORDINALS

1st	2nd	3rd	4th
first	second	third	fourth
5th	6th	21st	32nd
fifth	sixth	twenty-first	thirty-second

Miss Rose

Tan   Alain   Joe   Shantra   Miguel

Akiko

7th   6th   5th   4th   3rd   2nd   1st

1. Who is first? _____

2. Who is second? _____

3. Who is third? _____

4. Who is fifth? _____

5. Who is last? _____

See directions on page 19.

PLACE VALUES - 1

6	76	276
one-digit number	two-digit number	three-digit number

a. This is a four-digit number: **5,276**

b. We read this number: *five thousand, two hundred seventy-six.*

c. Each digit has a place in the number. Each place has a value.

5 , 2   7   6

thousands place hundreds place   tens place   ones place

d. The 6 is in the _____ place. Its value is 6.

e. The 7 is in the _____ place. Its value is 70.

f. The 2 is in the _____ place. Its value is 200.

g. The 5 is in the _____ place. Its value is 5,000.

h. There is a comma between the hundreds place and the _____ place.

Write the number that has:

i. 8 ones, 5 tens, 0 hundreds, 1 thousand. _____

PLACE VALUES - 2

a. This is a six digit number: **4 3 5, 6 2 9**
   Four hundred thirty-five thousand, six hundred twenty-nine.

$$4 \quad 3 \quad 5 \quad , \quad 6 \quad 2 \quad 9$$

hundred thousands place	ten thousands place	thousands place	hundreds place	tens place	ones place

b. The 5 is in the _____ place. Its value is 5,000.

c. The 3 is in the _____ place. Its value is 30,000.

d. The 4 is in the _____ place. Its value is 400,000.

e. A comma separates the hundreds place from the thousands place.

f. 729,012 = 700,000 + 20,000 + 9,000 + 000+ 10 + 2
   Seven hundred twenty-nine thousand, twelve.

g. 397,501 = _____

   _____

h. 407,869 = _____

   _____

HOW TO READ LARGE NUMBERS

We use commas to make large numbers easier to read.

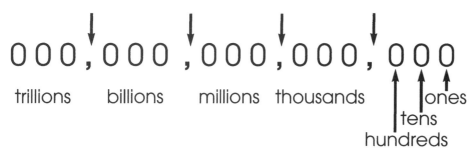

000,000,000,000,000

trillions   billions   millions   thousands   hundreds   tens   ones

Read these numbers

a. 222,222,222,222
    Two hundred twenty-two billion, two hundred twenty-two million,
    two hundred twenty-two thousand, two hundred twenty two

b.   333,333

c.   888,888,888

d.   555,555,555,555

e. 444,444,444,444,444

f.   111,111,111,111

g.   700,700,700,700

h.   203,203,203,203

i.   555,000,555,000

j.   32,406,008,200

READ AND WRITE LARGE NUMBERS

Write commas in the correct places in these numbers. The first is done for you.

a. 1,285   b. 48035   c. 68904

d. 431800   e. 10973000

f. 2420021527   g. 9674310530

Write the numbers.

a. <u>one thousand, two hundred eighty-five</u>

   _____

b. _____

   _____

c. _____

   _____

d. _____

   _____

e. _____

   _____

   _____

f. _____

   _____

          See directions on page 19.

DIFFERENT WAYS OF READING NUMBERS

756

1. Seven hundred fifty-six.

2. Seven fifty-six Oak Street. Room seven fifty six.

1,756

3. One thousand, seven hundred fifty-six.

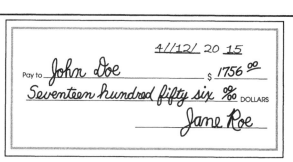

4. Seventeen hundred fifty-six dollars.

2012
1998
1861
1803
1776
1492

5. Seventeen fifty-six.

201 555 - 1756

6. Two-oh-one, five-five-five, one-seven-five-six.

Read these numbers:

a. 342

b.

c. 1,342

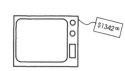

d.

e. October 10, 1342

f. (609) 555-1342

MATH TERMS

1, 2, 3, 4, 5, 6, 7, 8, 9 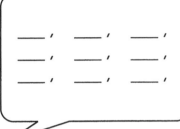 1. Count.	5, 10, 15, 20, 25, 30, 35, 40, 45, . . .  2. Count by fives.
__ , __ , __ , __ , __ , __ , __ , __ , __ , 3. Count by twos.	6 x 2 = 12 9 x 2 = 18 5 X ___ = ___ 4. Double.
a. ⟨617⟩ 716 921 b. 421 902 315 5. The least.	a. 925 543 ⟨1,022⟩ b. 99 200 132 6. The greatest.

7. Round off each number: 1,826   2,927   14,491

   a. to the nearest ten   **1,830**   _____   _____

   b. to the nearest hundred   **1,800**   _____   _____

   c. to the nearest thousand   **2,000**   _____   _____

    See directions on page 20.

DIFFERENT KINDS OF NUMBERS

one, two, three, four, five, six, seven, eight, nine…	first, second, third, fourth, fifth, sixth, seventh, eighth, ninth, tenth	1, 2, 3, 4, 5, 6, 7, 8, 9, 10…	I, II, III, IV, V, VI, VII, VIII, IX, X…
cardinal numbers	ordinal numbers	Arabic numerals	Roman numerals
2, 4, 6, 8, 10,…	1, 3, 5, 7, 9,…	$\frac{1}{2}$ $\frac{1}{3}$ $\frac{3}{4}$	$1\frac{1}{4}$ $2\frac{2}{3}$
even numbers	odd numbers	fractions	mixed numbers
.01 1.3	-2 -10	x y a + b	∞
decimals	negative numbers	unknown numbers	infinity

MATCH.

1. 11 13 15 17   _____   A. ordinal numbers

2. -4 -9 -12 -56   _____   B. Roman numerals

3. third fifth tenth   _____   C. fractions

4. XI IV XXVIII   _____   D. unknown numbers

5. 6 8 10 12   _____   E. negative numbers

6. .02 4.3 24.001   _____   F. even numbers

7. a + b = c   _____   G. odd numbers

8. $\frac{1}{2}$ $\frac{5}{6}$ $\frac{9}{10}$ _____   H. mixed numbers

                                   _____   I. decimal numbers

9. $3\frac{1}{3}$ $18\frac{1}{4}$

FRACTIONS - 1

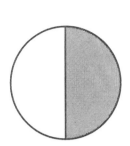 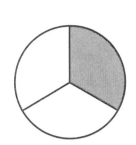 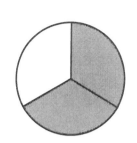 

| a.one-half | b. one-third | c. two-thirds | d. one (whole) |

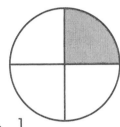 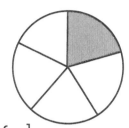 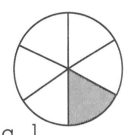 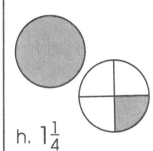

e. $\frac{1}{4}$
one-fourth
one-quarter

f. $\frac{1}{5}$
one-fifth

g. $\frac{1}{6}$
one-sixth

h. $1\frac{1}{4}$
one and
one fourth

Write the fraction and the words.

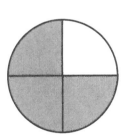 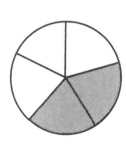 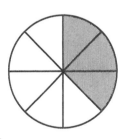 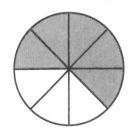

i. _____   j. _____   k. _____   l. _____

 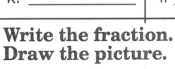

**Write the fraction.
Draw the picture.**

m. _____   n. _____   o. five -sixths   p. one and
one-third

See directions on page 20.

FRACTIONS - 2

a. The top number in a fraction is called the <u>numerator</u>. The bottom number is the <u>denominator</u>.

$$\frac{2}{3}$$

2 ← numerator

3 ← denominator

(two thirds)

b. These fractions have the same denominators. They have <u>common denominators.</u> The common denominator is <u>five</u>.

$$\frac{1}{5} \qquad \frac{3}{5} \qquad \frac{4}{5}$$

c. Draw lines to match the fractions that have common denominators.

1.

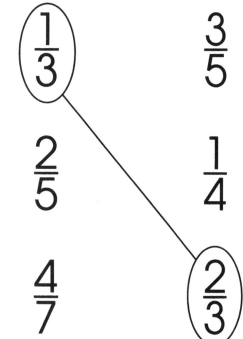

$\frac{1}{3}$	$\frac{3}{5}$
$\frac{2}{5}$	$\frac{1}{4}$
$\frac{4}{7}$	$\frac{2}{3}$

2.

$\frac{3}{4}$	$\frac{3}{8}$
$\frac{5}{6}$	$\frac{1}{4}$
$\frac{5}{8}$	$\frac{1}{6}$

DECIMAL NUMBERS

$\dfrac{1}{10}$

.1

a) point one
one tenth

$\dfrac{2}{100}$

.02

b) point oh two
point zero two
two hundredths

$1\dfrac{7}{10}$

1.7

c) one point seven
one and seven tenths

$3\dfrac{5}{100}$

3.05

d) three point oh five
three point zero five
three and five hundredths

$\dfrac{4}{1000}$

.004

e) point oh oh four
point zero zero four
four thousandths

$\dfrac{234}{1000}$

.234

f) point two three four
two hundred thirty-four
thousandths

3.5 million

g) three point five million
(3,500,000)

h) Write these decimals.

1. three tenths
2. one and four tenths
3. five hundredths
4. two and fifteen hundredths

1. _____   2. _____

3. _____   4. _____

See directions on page 20.

LINES

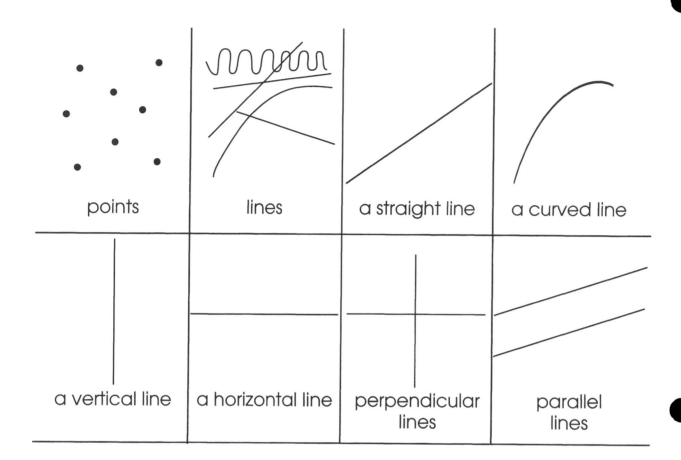

Draw:

a. a curved line

d. four points

b. a vertical line

e. a horizontal line

c. parallel lines

f. perpendicular lines

© 1995 by Elizabeth Claire and Barbara J. Haynes

ANGLES AND TRIANGLES

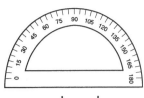

a protractor

ANGLES

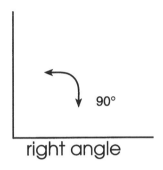

90°

right angle

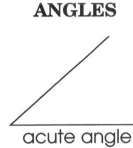

acute angle

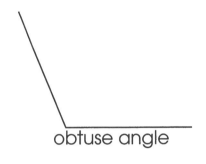

obtuse angle

TRIANGLES

equilateral
triangle

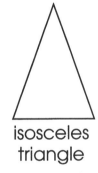

isosceles
triangle

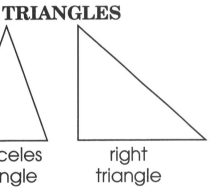

right
triangle

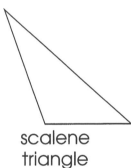

scalene
triangle

Match

1. A protractor _____

2. A right angle _____

3. An acute angle _____

4. An obtuse angle _____

5. An equilateral triangle _____

6. An isosceles triangle _____

7. A right triangle _____

8. A scalene triangle _____

A. has three equal sides.

B. has no equal sides.

C. has a right angle.

D. measures angles.

E. has two equal sides.

F. is larger than 90°

G. is 90°

H. is less than 90°

     See directions on page 20.

Name _____   Date _____

SHAPES

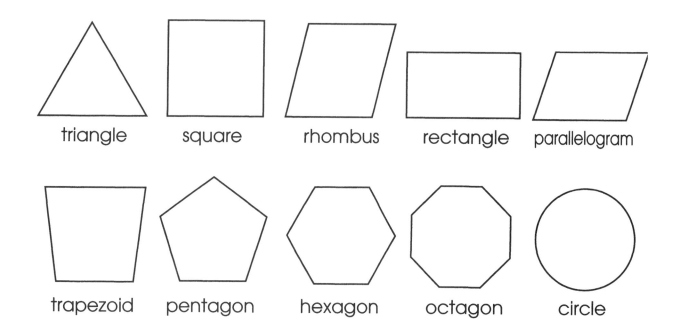

triangle   square   rhombus   rectangle   parallelogram

trapezoid   pentagon   hexagon   octagon   circle

SOLID SHAPES

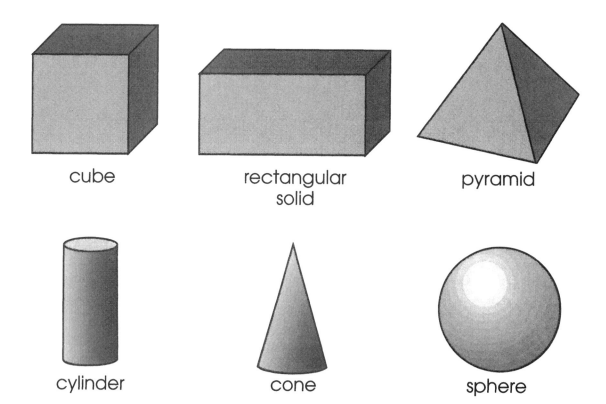

cube   rectangular solid   pyramid

cylinder   cone   sphere

See directions on page 000.   © 1995 by Elizabeth Claire and Barbara J. Haynes

CIRCLES

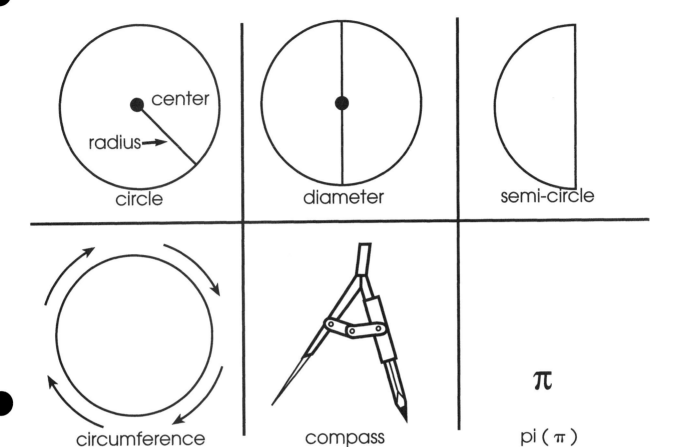

circle	diameter	semi-circle

circumference
360° (degrees)

compass

π

pi (π)

a. The diameter of a circle is two times the _____.

b. π = 3.14

c. π times the diameter equals the _____.

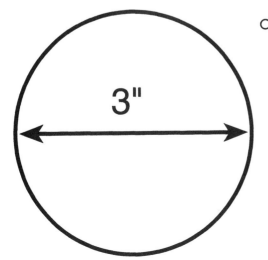

3"

d. 3.14 x 3 = _____"

π x D = C

3.14 X 3 = ___

See directions on page 20.

DRAW THE SHAPE OR LINE

1. a circle	2. three angles	3. a square	4. a triangle
5. a pentagon	6. a semi-circle	7. a right angle	8. an obtuse angle
9. a rectangle	10. a hexagon	11. a cube	12. a cylinder
13. a rhombus	14. a vertical line	15. a radius	16. a diameter

HOW LONG IS THIS PENCIL?

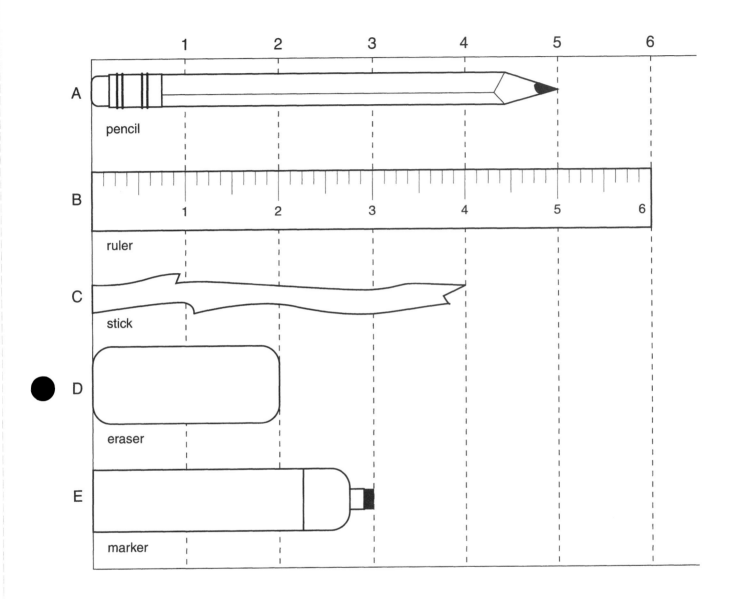

1. The pencil is ___ inches long.

2. The ruler is ____ _____ _____.

3. The stick ____ __ _____ _____.

4. ____ _____ _____ __ _____ _____.

5. _____.

See directions on page 21.

HOW TALL ARE THESE PEOPLE?

1. Joe is <u>five</u> feet tall.

2. Mei is _____ feet tall.

3. Mr. Wada is _____ _____ _____.

4. Miss Rose is <u>five feet</u>, <u>six inches</u> tall.

5. Akiko is _____ _____, _____ _____ tall.

6. Carmen _____.

7. Mr. Nichols _____.

LONG, WIDE, AND HIGH

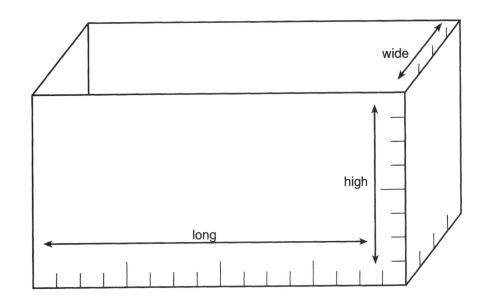

1. This box is _____**four**_____ inches long, _____ inch wide, and _____ inches high.

2. This paper is _____ inches long and _____ inches wide.

3. My desk is _____ inches long, _____ inches wide, and _____ inches high.

4. The teacher's desk is _____ inches long, _____ inches wide, and _____ inches high.

5. The classroom is _____ feet, _____ inches long, and _____ feet, _____ inches wide.

6. The hall is _____ feet, _____ inches long and _____ feet, _____ inches wide.

See directions on page 21.

Name _____ Date _____

MY MEASUREMENTS

1. I am _____ feet _____ inches tall.

2. My arm is _____ feet _____ inches long.

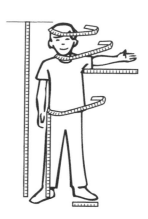

3. My leg is _____ feet _____ inches long.

4. My foot is _____ inches long.

5. My head is _____ inches around.

6. My neck is _____ inches around.

7. My waist is _____ inches around.

8. My ankle is _____ inches around.

9. My arm span is _____ feet _____ inches.

10. My longest step is _____ feet _____ inches.

See directions on page 21.   © 1995 by Elizabeth Claire and Barbara J. Haynes

CHANGE FEET TO INCHES

one foot = twelve inches	1 ft = 12 in.
in. = inch or inches	ft = foot or feet
" = inch or inches	' = foot or feet

1. 24 inches = ____ feet.

2. 36 inches = ____ feet.

3. 48 inches = ____ feet.

4. 12 inches = ____ foot.

5. 5 feet = ____ inches.

6. 2 feet = ____ inches.

7. 1 ft., 3 in. = ____ in.

8. 2 ft., 4 in. = ____ in.

9. 3' 2" = ____ "

10. 4' 1"= ____ "

  See directions on page 21.

MEASURING LIQUID - 1

teaspoon
(tsp)

tablespoon
(tbs)

cup
(c)

ounce
(oz)

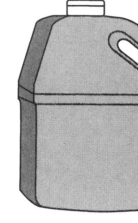

pint
(pt)

quart
(qt)

half gallon
(1/2 gal)

gallon
(gal)

3 teaspoons = 1 tablespoon

2 tablespoons = 1 ounce

8 ounces = 1 cup

2 cups = 1 pint

4 quarts = 1 gallon

32 ounces = 1 quart

4 cups = 1 quart

2 quarts = 1 half gallon

2 pints = 1 quart

See directions on page 21

MEASURING LIQUIDS - 2

This table shows the relationship between cups, pints, quarts, gallons, and half gallons.

cup	cup	cup	cup	cup	cup	cup	cup	cup	cup	cup	cup	cup	cup	cup	cup
pint		pint		pint		pint		pint		pint		pint		pint	
quart				quart				quart				quart			
half gallon								half gallon							
gallon															

Write the missing word or number.

a. Two cups = 1 _____.

b. Two pints = 1 _____.

c. Four _____ = 1 quart.

d. Four _____ = 1 gallon.

e. 1 gallon = _____ cups.

f. 1 gallon = _____ pints.

g. 1 gallon = _____ quarts.

h. 8 cups = _____ quarts.

i. 16 cups = _____ pints = _____ quarts = 1 _____.

See directions on page 21.

MEASURING LIQUIDS - 3

1. Which holds more, a gallon or a pint? ___**a gallon**___

2. Which holds more, a pint or a cup? _____

3. Which holds more, a pint or a quart?_____

4. Which holds more, a teaspoon or a tablespoon? _____

5. Which holds more, an ounce or a tablespoon? _____

6. How many tablespoons are in an ounce? _____

7. How many ounces are in a cup? _____

8. How many ounces are in a pint? _____

9. How many ounces are in a quart? _____

10. How many cups are in a quart? _____

11. How many quarts are in a gallon? _____

12. How many cups are in two pints? _____

13. How many cups are in two quarts? _____

See directions on page 21.

HOW MUCH DO THESE THINGS WEIGH? - 1

a. book

b. boy

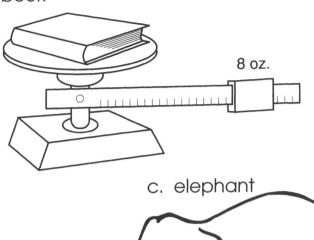

8 oz.

c. elephant

1. The _____ weighs 8 ounces.

2. The _____ weighs 110 pounds.

3. The _____ weighs 2 tons.

WEIGHT

16 ounces = 1 pound   oz. = ounce

2000 pounds = 1 ton   lb. = pound

                               T. = ton

Note: An ounce of liquid is not the same as an ounce of weight.

See directions on page 21.

HOW MUCH DO THESE THINGS WEIGH? - 2

Guess the weight of each object. Write down your guess. Then weigh the object. Write down the correct weight.

Object	My Guess	Actual weight (ounces/pounds)
math book		

Write sentences about the things you weighed.
Example:

My math book weighs 14 ounces. _____

_____

_____

_____

_____

_____

_____

_____

_____

WHERE IS THE UNITED STATES OF AMERICA? - 1

1. This is the <u>continent</u> of North America.

2. The United States is a <u>country</u> in North America.

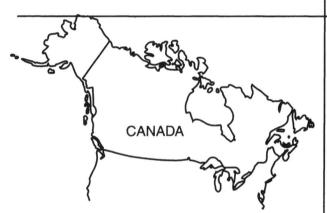

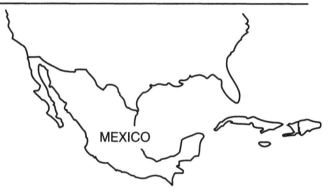

3. The United States has two neighbors. Canada is to the north.

4. Mexico is to the south.

5. The United States touches two oceans. The Atlantic Ocean is on the east, and the Pacific Ocean is on the west.

Pacific Ocean

Atlantic Ocean

Gulf of Mexico

6. The Gulf of Mexico is on the south.

    See directions on page 23.

WHERE IS THE UNITED STATES OF AMERICA? - 2

I. KEY WORDS: Write these words in your language. Find the words in the story and underline them.

united	states	continent	country
neighbors	Canada	Mexico	north
south	touch	ocean	Atlantic
east	pacific	west	Gulf

II. Complete the sentences.

1. North America is a _____

2. The United States is a _____ in North America.

3. The Atlantic Ocean is on the _____ and the
   _____ Ocean is on the west.

4. _____ is to the north.

5. Mexico is to the _____.

6. Canada and Mexico are _____ of the United
   States.

THE FIFTY STATES - 1

1. There are fifty states in the United States.

2. Two states do not touch the other states.

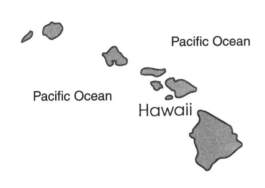

3. Hawaii is a group of islands in the Pacific Ocean.

4. Alaska is north and west of Canada. It is the largest state in the United States.

5. Puerto Rico is part of the United States. It is not a state.

6. Washington, D.C., is the capital of the United States.

          See directions on page 23.

THE FIFTY STATES - 2

KEY WORDS: Write these words in your language. Find the words in the story and underline them.

fifty	touch	Hawaii	group
islands	Alaska	large	larger
largest	Puerto Rico	Washington, D.C.	capital

Fill in the blanks.

1. There are _____ states in the United States.

2. Two states do not touch the other states. They are _____ and _____.

3. Hawaii is a group of _____ in the Pacific Ocean.

4. Alaska is north and west of _____.

5. The largest state is _____.

6. Puerto Rico is part of the _____.

7. The capital of the United States is_____.

THE MAP OF THE UNITED STATES

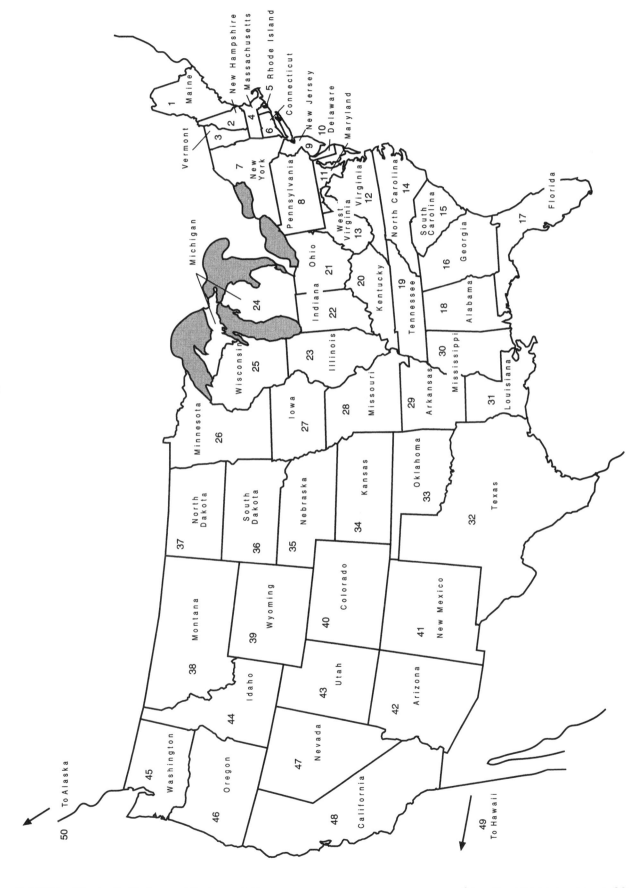

See directions on page 23.

THE MAP OF THE UNITED STATES - 2

Look at the map and answer these questions.

1. How many states are in the United States? _____

2. I live in the state of _____
   (Color it orange.)

3. The states that touch my state are

   _____

   _____

   (Color them yellow.)

4. Which states touch the Pacific Ocean?

   _____

   _____

   _____

   _____

5. Which states touch the Atlantic Ocean?

   _____

   _____

   _____

   _____

6. Which states touch Canada?

   _____

   _____

   _____

THE MAP OF THE UNITED STATES - 3

7. Which states touch Mexico?

_____

_____

8. Which states touch the Gulf of Mexico?

_____

_____

9. Find Nevada. Go east to Kansas. Which states do you cross?

_____

_____

10. Find New Jersey. Go west to California. Which states do you cross?

_____

_____

_____

_____

11. Find North Dakota. Go south to Texas. Which states do you cross?

_____

_____

12. Find Louisiana. Go north to Minnesota. Which states do you cross?

_____

_____

        See directions on page 23.

THE MAP OF THE UNITED STATES - 4

13. Which states' names begin with the word "New"?

_____

_____

_____

_____

14. Which states' names begin with "North," "South," or "West?"

_____

_____

_____

_____

15. On another sheet of paper, trace the map of the United States. Write in the names of the states.

16. On another sheet of paper, write the names of the states in alphabetical order.

17. Learn the capitals of the states.

18. Find picture books on these topics. Write a short report on each book.

    The United States: Geography
    North America
    New England states
    Atlantic states
    the South
    the Midwest
    the Southwest
    the Central Plains
    the Northwest
    Alaska
    Hawaii
    (My state) _____

THE STATES AND THEIR CAPITALS

Find these states on the map.

STATE	CAPITAL	STATE	CAPITAL
Alabama	Montgomery	Montana	Helena
Alaska	Juneau	Nebraska	Lincoln
Arizona	Phoenix	Nevada	Carson City
Arkansas	Little Rock	New York	Albany
California	Sacramento	New Hampshire	Concord
Colorado	Denver	New Mexico	Santa Fe
Connecticut	Hartford	New Jersey	Trenton
Delaware	Dover	North Carolina	Raleigh
Florida	Tallahassee	North Dakota	Bismarck
Georgia	Atlanta	Ohio	Columbus
Hawaii	Honolulu	Oklahoma	Oklahoma City
Idaho	Boise	Oregon	Salem
Illinois	Springfield	Pennsylvania	Harrisburg
Indiana	Indianapolis	Rhode Island	Providence
Iowa	Des Moines	South Carolina	Columbia
Kansas	Topeka	South Dakota	Pierre
Kentucky	Frankfort	Tennessee	Nashville
Louisiana	Baton Rouge	Texas	Austin
Maine	Augusta	Utah	Salt Lake City
Maryland	Annapolis	Vermont	Montpelier
Massachusetts	Boston	Virginia	Richmond
Michigan	Lansing	Washington	Olympia
Minnesota	Saint Paul	West Virginia	Charleston
Mississippi	Jackson	Wisconsin	Madison
Missouri	Jefferson City	Wyoming	Cheyenne
			District of Columbia

  See directions on page 23.

UNITED STATES WORD SEARCH

Find and circle the names of the states in this puzzle

```
N S O R E G O N E W M E X I C O S O U T S
E O M W Y O M I N G I N D I A N A L T E O
N K E N T U C K Y A O M A L L A S K E V U
C O L O R A D O N O W I S L I O K L N I T
H K L O U I S I A N A N P I F E N M N R H
P L M I S S O U R I I N A N O P X A E G D
E A S Y A L U N B A N E T O R E R R S I A
N H A W L U T E X M O S E I N N H Y S N K
M O L A A W H W I S C O N S I N O L E I O
A M A S S A C H U S E T T S A S D A E A T
I A B H K R A A C I D A H O M Y E N S M A
N V A I A I R M O N T A N A G L I D N I F
E W M N R Z O P N E W Y O R K V S E M S L
B M A G K O L S N W H O R N E A L L I S O
R O B T A N I H E J A S T K V N A A C I R
A N A O N A N I C E W S H T I I N W H S I
S T U N S T A R T R A H D E R A D A I S D
K A N S A S D E I S I A A X G E O R G I A
A N K O S T A M C E I O K A I N T E A P S
M A S U T A H A U Y N A O S N E B R N P A
I N E V A D A K T W E S T V I R G I N I A
N O R T H C A R O L I N A X A A K O H I O
```

THE UNITED STATES: LAND AND WATER - 1

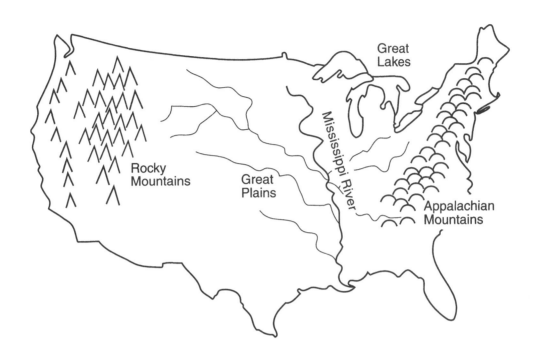

1. The United States has many mountains. The Rocky Mountains are in the West.

2. The Appalachian Mountains are in the East.

3. The middle of the United States is flat. This is the Great Plains.

4. There are five Great Lakes.

5. There are many large rivers. The longest is the Mississippi River.

Color the Rocky Mountains brown.
Color the Appalachian Mountains orange.
Color the Great Plains green.
Color the Great Lakes blue.

　　　　See directions on page 24.

THE UNITED STATES: LAND AND WATER - 2

KEY WORDS: **Write these words in your language. Find the words in the story and underline them.**

mountains	rock	Rocky
lake	river	plains
West	Appalachian	the
East	central	flat
longest	river	Mississippi

Write the missing words.

1. The mountains in the West are the _____
   Mountains.

2. The _____ Mountains are in the East.

3. The longest _____ is the Mississippi.

4. There are _____ Great Lakes.

5. In which states are the Rocky Mountains?

   _____

   _____

6. Which states touch the Great Lakes?

   _____

   _____

FACTS ABOUT THE UNITED STATES: QUIZ

I. Match.

1. continent _____   A. the United States

2. country _____   B. Washington, D.C.

3. capital _____   C. Atlantic and Pacific

4. oceans _____   D. North America

5. largest state _____   E. Canada and Mexico

6. island state _____   F. Hawaii

7. U.S. neighbors _____   G. Alaska

8. mountains in the West _____   H. Great Plains

9. mountains in the East _____   I. Appalachians

10. longest river _____   J. Rockies

11. There are five _____   K. Mississippi

12. the flat land in the _____ L. Great Lakes
    middle of the U.S.

          See directions on page 24.

THE PEOPLE OF THE UNITED STATES - 1

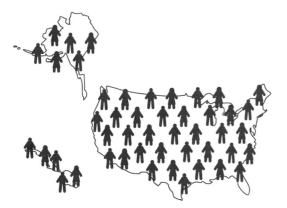

1. Three hundred five million people live in the United States. The people are called Americans.

2. Most Americans live in or near big cities.

3. Some people live in small towns or on farms.

4. Most Americans are immigrants or the descendants of immigrants.

5. The city with the most people is New York City.

6. Other big cities are Los Angeles, Chicago, Houston, and San Diego.

THE PEOPLE OF THE UNITED STATES - 2

KEY WORDS: Write these words in your language. Find the words in the story and underline them.

hundred	million	most
people	near	city, cities
some	town	farm
immigrants	descendants	New York City
Chicago	Houston	San Diego

1. How many people live in the United States?
   a. 30,000
   b. 3,000,000
   c. 305,000,000
   d. 350,000

2. Where do most Americans live?
   a. in small towns
   b. on farms
   c. in New York City
   d. in or near big cities

3. An immigrant is a person who came from another country to live in the United States. A descendent is a child, grandchild, great grandchild, etc.

   Most Americans are _____ or the
   descendants of _____ .

4. The city with the most people is
   a. Los Angeles
   b. New York City
   c. Houston
   d. Chicago

5. Chicago is
   a. a big city
   b. a small town
   c. near New York City
   d. in Canada.

Find picture books on these topics. Write a report.

Washington, D.C., New York City, Los Angeles, Chicago, your city or town

   See directions on page 24.

THE LEADERS OF THE UNITED STATES - 1

1. This is _____
   (He/She) is the president of
   the United States.

2. This is _____
   (He/She) is the vice president
   of the United States.

3. The president lives in the
   White House.

4. The United States is a
   democracy. The people
   vote to elect the president.

5. There is an election for
   president every four years.
   The election is in November.

6. People elect representatives
   to make laws.

See directions on page 24.

THE LEADERS OF THE UNITED STATES - 2

KEY WORDS: Write these words in your language. Find the words in the story and underline them.

president	vice president	White House
democracy	elect	vote
election	every four years	representatives
make laws		

Answer the questions.

1. Who is the president of the United States?

_____

2. Who is the vice president?

_____

3. Where does the president live?

_____

4. When is the election for president?

_____

5. Who elects the president?

_____

6. Who makes the laws for the country?

_____

Find picture books on these topics. Write a report.

the president, the White House, elections, Congress

SYMBOLS OF THE UNITED STATES - 1

1. This is the Statue of Liberty. It is on an island in New York Harbor.

2. This is the flag of the United States. It is red, white and blue. It has thirteen stripes and fifty stars.

3. This is Uncle Sam. He is a symbol of the government of the United States.

4. The bald eagle is the national bird.

O—h say can you see –
By the dawn's early light,

5. "The Star-Spangled Banner" is the national song of the United States. It is a song about the flag.

6. This is the Liberty Bell. It's in Independence Hall in Philadelphia, Pennsylvania.

SYMBOLS OF THE UNITED STATES - 2

KEY WORDS: Write these words in your language. Find the words in the story and underline them.

symbol	statue	liberty
harbor	flag	red
white	blue	star
thirteen	stripe	uncle
government	eagle	bald

Answer the questions.

1. Where is the Statue of Liberty?

   _____

2. What color is the flag of the United States?

   _____

3. The United States flag has _____ stars and _____ stripes.

4. Who is Uncle Sam? _____

   _____

5. The _____ is the national bird.

6. What is the national song of the United States?

   _____

7. Where is the Liberty Bell?_____

Find picture books on these topics. Write a report.

the Statue of Liberty, the flag of the United States, Uncle Sam, The Star Spangled Banner, the Liberty Bell

     See directions on page 24.

Name _____   Date _____

MY STATE

Look at a map of your state. Ask someone to help you with the questions.

1. I live in the state of _____.

2. My state's nickname is _____.

3. The capital of my state is _____.

4. The largest city in my state is _____.

5. The governor of my state is _____.

6. _____ people live in my state.

7. The states that touch my state are

_____

_____

8. The highest mountains in my state are

_____

9. The longest river in my state is _____.

10. My state is well known for

_____

_____

_____

Find picture books about your state. Write a report.

See directions on page 000.

Name _____ Date _____ R135

MY TOWN

1. I live in _____.

2. It is in the county of _____, in the state of
   _____.

3. _____ people live in my town.

4. _____ is the mayor of my town.

5. Some interesting facts about my town:

   _____

   _____

   _____

   _____

   _____

   _____

   _____

   _____

   _____

   _____

   _____

   _____

   _____

   _____

Find picture books about your town. Write a report.

See directions on page 25.

THE FIRST PEOPLE IN AMERICA - 1

1. For a very long time, there were no people in America.

2. About twenty thousand years ago, the first people came. They came from Asia.

3. After many, many years, there were people living all over North and South America. They spoke many different languages.

See directions on page 25.

THE FIRST PEOPLE IN AMERICA - 2

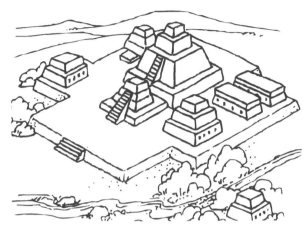

4. Some of these people lived in great cities.

5. Some were farmers and lived in small villages.

6. Other groups of people did not live in one place. They were hunters. They moved to follow the animals that they hunted.

7. We call all of these people Native Americans.

See directions on page 25.

THE FIRST PEOPLE IN AMERICA - 3

KEY WORDS: Write these words in your language. Find the words in the story and underline them.

years ago	cities	move
Asia	farmers	speak/spoke
Native Americans	villages	languages
groups	hunters	no
different	homes	

Write the missing words.

1. For a very long time, there were _____ people in America.

2. About _____ years ago, the first people came.

3. They came from _____.

4. After many, many years, there were people living all over _____ and _____ America.

5. Some people lived in great _____.

6. Some were farmers and lived in _____.

7. Hunters moved when the _____ moved.

8. We call all these people _____ _____.

Find picture books on Native Americans. Write a report.

Eastern Woodlands Indians: Iroquois   Plains Indians: Dakota
Pueblo Indians: Ute, Navajo   Northwest Indians
Aztec; Mayans; Inca   Eskimo, Inuit

© 1995 by Elizabeth Claire and Barbara J. Haynes

COLUMBUS COMES TO AMERICA - 1

1. In 1492, three ships came to America. They came from Spain.

2. Their leader was Christopher Columbus. Columbus was looking for a way to go to China and the Indies.

3. Columbus thought he was in the Indies. When he met the Native Americans, he called them "Indians."

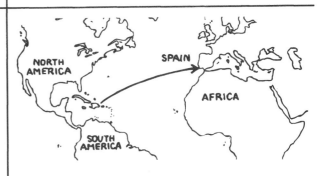

4. Columbus went back to Spain. He told everyone about the land and the people that he had found.

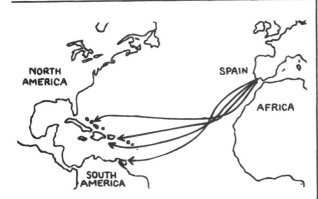

5. Columbus made four trips to America. He claimed the land for Spain.

6. Many Spanish people came after Columbus. They started Spanish colonies in America.

   See directions on page 25.

COLUMBUS COMES TO AMERICA - 2

KEY WORDS: Write these words in your language. Find the
words in the story and underline them.

ships	Spain	leader
Christopher Columbus	China	Indies
think/thought	tell/told	find/found
trips	claim	colony

Complete the sentences.

1. Christopher Columbus came to America in the year _____.

2. Columbus was looking for a way to go to
   _____ and _____

3. Columbus called the people in America
   _____ because he thought he was
   in the Indies.

4. Columbus made _____ trips to America.
   a. four   b. two
   c. three   d. no

5. Columbus claimed the land in America for _____

Find picture books on these topics. Write a report.

The Explorers and Discoverers

Christopher Columbus, Amerigo Vespucci
Hernando Cortes, Montezuma
Cabeza de Vaca Francisco Coronado,
Hernando de Soto, Ponce de Leon

COLONIES IN NORTH AMERICA - 1

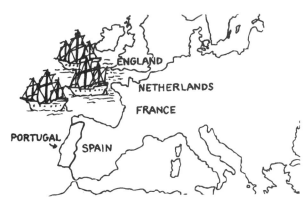

1. Soon people from other countries came to America. These people started many new colonies.

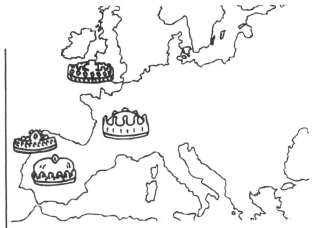

2. The colonies were owned by kings and queens in Europe.

3. There were Spanish colonies in Mexico, Florida, and Central and South America.

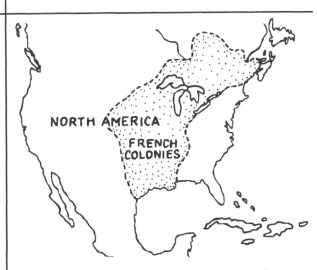

4. There were French colonies from Canada to Louisiana.

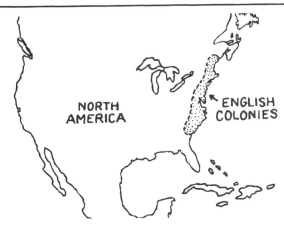

5. There were English colonies on the East Coast of North America.

6. The Dutch had a colony called New Netherlands. It was on the East Coast, too.

 See directions on page 25.

COLONIES IN NORTH AMERICA - 2

KEY WORDS: Write these words in your language. Find the words in the story and underline them.

kings	queens	Europe
Mexico	Florida	Central
Louisiana	coast	the Netherlands

1. The colonies were owned by _____ and _____ in Europe.

2. Spain had colonies in _____, _____ and _____.

3. France had colonies from _____ to _____.

4. There were English colonies on the East Coast of _____.

5. The Netherlands had a colony on the _____ too.

Find picture books on these topics. Write a report.

Jaques Cartier, Samuel de Champlain
Henry Hudson, John Cabot, Peter Minuit
Montreal, New Amsterdam, St. Augustine
New Orleans

WHY DID PEOPLE COME TO AMERICA? - 1

1. Some people came to America to look for gold.

2. Some people came to trade with the Native Americans.

3. Some people came to teach the Native Americans about Christianity.

4. Some people came for religious freedom.

5. Some poor people wanted to come to America for a better life. They did not have money for the trip. They became servants for seven years. After seven years, they were free and got land.

6. Some people did not want to come to America. They were brought here as slaves from Africa. The slaves worked all their lives. Most of them never became free.

See directions on page 25.

WHY DID PEOPLE COME TO AMERICA? - 2

KEY WORDS: Write these words in your language. Find the words in the story and underline them.

gold	trade	teach
Christianity	religious	freedom
poor	servants	free
slaves	never	

Write the missing words.

1. Some people came to America to look for _____.

2. Some people came to trade with the _____
   _____.

3. Some people came to teach the Native Americans about
   _____.

4. Some people came for _____ freedom.

5. Some poor people came to America as _____.

6. Some Africans were brought to America as _____.

Find picture books on these topics. Write a report.

Saint Augustine, Florida
Hernando Cortes; Montezuma
Bartolome de las Casas
Marquette and Joliet
the slave trade

© 1995 by Elizabeth Claire and Barbara J. Haynes

THE THIRTEEN ENGLISH COLONIES - 1

1. The first English colony was Jamestown, in Virginia. It was started in 1609.

2. In 1620, other English people came. They sailed on a ship called the Mayflower. They were the Pilgrims.

3. The Pilgrims wanted to have their own church. They started a colony at Plymouth, in Massachusetts.

4. In 1664 England took New Netherlands from the Dutch. They changed the name to New York.

5. By 1732 there were thirteen English colonies: Massachusetts, New Hampshire, Connecticut, Rhode Island, New York, New Jersey, Pennsylvania, Delaware, Maryland, Virginia, North Carolina, South Carolina, and Georgia

New Hampshire
Massachusetts
New York
Rhode Island
Connecticut
Pennsylvania
New Jersey
Delaware
Maryland
Virginia
North Carolina
South Carolina
Georgia

See directions on page 25.

THE THIRTEEN ENGLISH COLONIES - 2

KEY WORDS: Write these words in your language. Find the words in the story and underline them.

colony	Jamestown	start
Pilgrim	church	Mayflower
Plymouth	Dutch	change

Match

1. The first English colony _____   A. wanted religious freedom

2. The Pilgrims _____   B. English name for New Netherlands

3. the Mayflower _____   C. Jamestown

4. New York _____   D. ship the Pilgrims came in.

5. What are the names of the thirteen English colonies?

_____

_____

_____

_____

_____

_____

Find picture books on these topics. Write a report.

Jamestown, Virginia, The Story of Pocahantas
The Pilgrims, Plymouth, the Mayflower, Squanto, the first Thanksgiving
William Penn, the Quakers, Philadelphia, Benjamin Franklin

AMERICANS HAVE TROUBLE WITH ENGLAND - 1

1. From 1756 to 1763, England was at war with France.

2. England won the war. Then France had to give Canada and the land east of the Mississippi River to England.

3. The war cost a lot of money. England wanted the American colonies to pay for the war.

4. England made new laws and new taxes for the colonists.

5. Americans could not help to make the laws so they did not want to pay the taxes.

6. The king punished the colonists. The Americans became very angry at the king.

7. In 1775, a war began.

See directions on page 25.

AMERICANS HAVE TROUBLE WITH ENGLAND - 2

KEY WORDS: Write these words in your language. Find the words in the story and underline them.

trouble	war	win/won	leave/left
cost	pay	laws	

1. From 1756 to 1763, England was at war with _____.

2. _____ won the war.

3. France had to give _____and the land east of the Mississippi River to England.

4. England wanted the American colonists to _____for the war.

5. England made new laws and new _____ for the colonists.

6. Americans could not help make the laws so they did _____ want to pay the taxes.

7. The king punished the _____. The Americans became very _____ at the king.

8. In _____ a war began.

Find picture books on these topics. Write a report.

Life in the colonies
Crispus Attucks
The Boston Massacre

The Boston Tea Party
Paul Revere
Lexington and Concord

THE BIRTH OF THE UNITED STATES - 1

1. A group of American leaders held a meeting. They met in the city of Philadelphia.

2. They talked about the war with England. "Let's fight for independence," they said. "Let's be free from England and King George."

3. One of the leaders was Thomas Jefferson. He wrote a paper that said that the colonies did not belong to England anymore. That paper is called the Declaration of Independence.

4. The other leaders signed the Declaration on July 4, 1776. That day was the birthday of the United States.

5. Another leader was George Washington. He became the general of the American army.

6. The War for Independence lasted for many years. It was called the American Revolutionary War.

      See directions on page 25.

THE BIRTH OF THE UNITED STATES - 2

KEY WORDS: Write these words in your language. Find the
words in the story and underline them.

group	leaders	hold a meeting
Philadelphia	fight/fought	independence
King George	Thomas Jefferson	Declaration
sign/signed	birthday	general
army	Revolution	

Fill in the blanks.

1. A group of American leaders met in the city of
   _____.

2. They talked about the war with England. "Let's fight for
   _____." they said.

3. Let's be free from England and _____ _____.

4. _____ wrote a paper that said the
   colonies did not belong to England anymore.

5. That paper is called the Declaration of _____.

6. The leaders signed the Declaration of Independence on July 4,
   _____. That day is the birthday of _____.

7. _____ was the general of the
   American army.

Find picture books on these topics. Write a report.

Benjamin Franklin, Patrick Henry, Nathan Hale,
George Washington, Thomas Jefferson
The Declaration of Independence
the American Revolution, Thomas Paine

See directions on page 25.

THE NEW GOVERNMENT OF THE UNITED STATES - 1

1. At last, England stopped fighting. The colonies were free. They were now independent states.

2. Some of the leaders wanted George Washington to be king.

3. "No," said Washington. "Let us have a democracy. Let's have government by the people, not by a king."

4. The leaders wanted a strong country. They wrote a plan for a new government. This plan was the Constitution.

5. George Washington was elected to be the first president. He was a very good president. He is called the "father of his country."

6. Thomas Jefferson was the third president. He was an important president too.

 See directions on page 000.

THE NEW GOVERNMENT OF THE UNITED STATES - 2

KEY WORDS: **Write these words in your language. Find the words in the story and underline them.**

at last	stop	democracy
strong	plan	
government	Constitution	elect
first	third	

1. After the war, some of the leaders wanted George Washington to be _____.

2. A democracy means government by the _____, not by a king or queen.

3. The plan for the new government of the United States was called the _____.

4. _____ was elected to be the first president of the United States.

5. George Washington is called the "_____ of his country."

6. Thomas _____ was elected to be the third president of the United States.

Find picture books on these topics. Write a report.

The Constitution   The Bill of Rights

See directions on page 25.

EARLY AMERICAN HISTORY: QUIZ

Write the letter of the best match.

1. The first people in America _____

2. Christopher Columbus _____

3. Spain, France, England, and the Netherlands _____

4. The first English colony was _____

5. The Pilgrims came to America _____

6. By 1732, there were _____

7. Thomas Jefferson _____

8. The Declaration of Independence was signed on _____

9. George Washington was _____

10. The United States is a _____

11. The Constitution is _____

ANSWERS

A. wrote the Declaration of Independence.

B. the plan for the government.

C. came from Asia 20,000 years ago.

D. to have religious freedom.

E. the general of the American army, the first president of the United States, and the "father of his country."

F. thirteen English colonies

G. democracy.

H. came to America in 1492.

I. all had colonies in North America.

J. July 4, 1776.

K. Jamestown, in Virginia

 See directions on page 25.

EARLY AMERICAN HISTORY: CROSSWORD PUZZLE

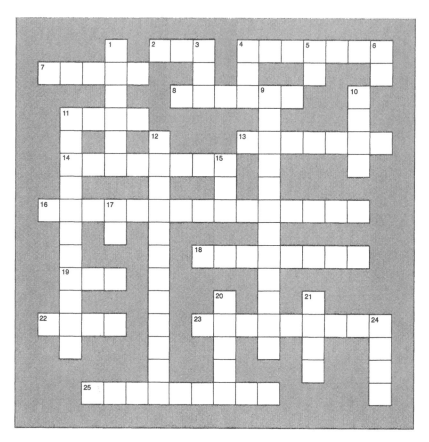

ACROSS

2. Rule; obey the ___.
4. Person who came to America for religious freedom.
7. People from New Netherlands
8. Country that had colonies from Canada to Louisiana.
11. Open the ___ and come in.
13. Country that had 13 colonies on the East Coast of America.
14. Lands that are owned by another country.
16. The first people in America.
18. He came to America in 1492.
19. Money that people pay to the government of a country.
22. Yellow metal that is used for money.
23. A government by the people.
25. The first English colony.

DOWN

1. A place to learn.
3. Americans fought a ____ for independence from England.
4. You can write with this.
5. Move.
6. I.
9. The plan of the government.
10. A leader of a country, not elected by the people.
11. & 12. Thomas Jefferson wrote the _____ of _____.
15. "Oh say, can you _____?"
17. Not out.
20. Hi.
21. Not a slave.
24. 365 days.

See directions on page 25.   © 1995 by Elizabeth Claire and Barbara J. Haynes

THE STORY OF MY NATIVE COUNTRY

1. My native country is _____.

2. It is in (near) the continent of _____.

3. My country's neighbors are: _____

   _____

4. My county touches the _____ (Ocean/Sea/Gulf)

5. The language people speak there is _____.

6. _____ people live in my country.

7. Most of the people live (in large cities, in villages, on farms).

8. The largest city in my country is _____.

9. The capital of my country is _____.

10. The leader of my country is _____.

11. Some interesting things about my country are:

    _____

    _____

    _____

    _____

    _____

    _____

    _____

    _____

  See directions on page 25.

THE THREE BRANCHES OF GOVERNMENT - 1

1. This tree has three branches.

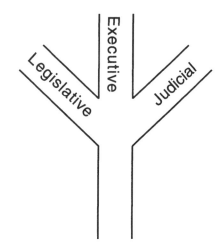

2. The government of the United States has three branches too.

3. Congress makes the laws. This is the legislative branch.

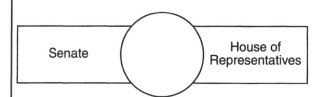

4. Congress has two parts: the Senate and the House of Representatives.

5. Each state elects two senators. Senators are elected for six years.

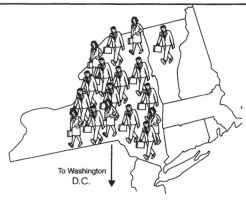

6. States with many people elect many representatives. States with few people elect only one representative. Representatives are elected for two years.

See directions on page 25

THE THREE BRANCHES OF GOVERNMENT - 2

KEY WORDS: Write these words in your language. Find the words in the story and underline them.

branch	government	congress
law	legislative	senate
representative	few	only

Fill in the blanks.

1. The government of the United States has _____ branches.

2. Congress makes the _____.

3. Congress is part of the _____ branch of the government.

4. Congress has two parts, the _____ and the House of _____.

5. There are _____ senators from each state.

6. Senators are elected for _____ years.

7. States with many people send many _____ to Congress.

8. The senators from my state are _____and _____.

9. Representatives are elected for _____ years.

10. The representative from my area is _____.

Find information on these topics. Write a report.

Congress   how laws are made

                 See directions on page 25.

THE THREE BRANCHES OF GOVERNMENT - 3

1. The president is the chief of the executive branch of the government. The executive branch enforces the laws.

2. The executive branch has many departments. The chiefs of the important departments are part of the president's <u>cabinet</u>.

3. When there is a question about the laws, people go to court. The courts interpret the laws. The courts are the judicial branch of the government.

4. The highest court in the United States is called the Supreme Court.

5. The judges are not elected. The president appoints Supreme Court judges for life.

See directions on page 25.   © 1995 by Elizabeth Claire and Barbara J. Haynes

THE THREE BRANCHES OF GOVERNMENT - 4

KEY WORDS: Write these words in your language. Find the
words in the story and underline them.

chief	executive	department
enforce	decide	court
interpret	judicial	Supreme
appoint	judge	defense

1. The president is the chief of the _____
   branch of the government.

2. The executive branch _____ the laws.

3. The executive branch has _____ departments.

4. The chiefs of the important departments are part of the
   president's _____.

5. The courts _____ the laws.

6. The courts are the _____ branch of the
   government.

7. The highest court in the United States is called the
   _____ Court.

8. The president _____ the judges of the Supreme
   Court.

Find picture books on these topics. Write a report.

The president   The Supreme Court

          See directions on page 25.

THE THREE BRANCHES OF GOVERNMENT - 5

I. Write each word below in its correct column.

LEGISLATIVE	EXECUTIVE	JUDICIAL
	president	

✔president   Congress   Supreme Court
senators   make laws   interpret laws
enforce laws   representatives   vice president
judge   cabinet
decides if someone has broken a law

II. How long are their terms? Match.

1. president____   a. two years

2. Senator____   b. four years

3. Representative____   c. six years

4. Supreme Court Justice ____   d. life

See directions on page 25.

AMERICANS HAVE MANY RIGHTS

1. People in the United States have many rights.

2. We have freedom of religion. We may go to any church.

3. We have freedom of speech. We may say what we think.

4. We have freedom of the press. A newspaper may print news about anything.

5. Police may not enter our house without a reason.

6. A person has the right to a trial by a jury if he or she is accused of breaking the law.

    See directions on page 25.

AMERICANS HAVE MANY RESPONSIBILITIES

1. Obey the law.

2. Respect the rights of other people.

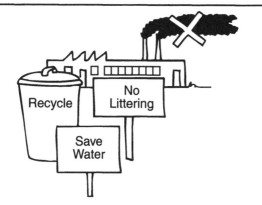

3. Take care of the environment.

4. Work and pay taxes.

5. Become educated. Learn about our country, its history and government.

6. Vote in elections.

See directions on page 26.

IMPORTANT PLACES AND TELEPHONE NUMBERS

1. My school's address _____

2. The school telephone number is _____

3. There is a public library at _____
   I can get a library card. Then I may borrow books for free.

4. The fire station is at _____

5. To report a fire, call _____

6. The police station is at _____

7. To call the police, call _____

8. There is a hospital emergency room at

   _____

9. Call _____ to get help in an emergency.

10. My phone number is (_____) _____.

11. My address is _____

    _____.

 See directions on page 27.

TIME ZONES

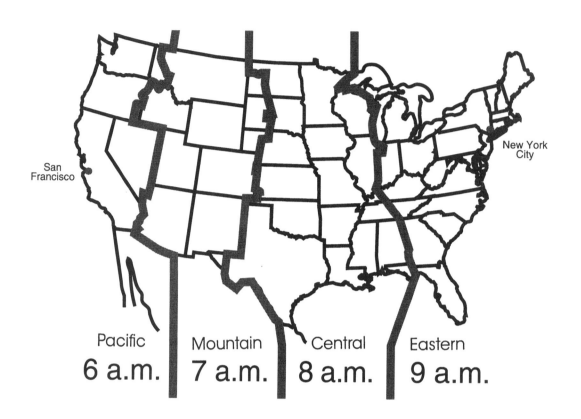

The United States is a very large country. There are four time zones in the continental United States. When it is nine a.m. in the morning in New York City, it is only six a.m. in San Francisco.

See directions on page 28.

CONVERSION TABLES
U.S. and Metric Systems
of Weights and Measurements

The United States uses a very old system of measurement.
The conversion tables below show how the U.S. system
compares with the metric system.
(See pages R106 to R114 for practice with the U.S. system)

U.S. to Metric

Distance

1 inch (in)	2.54 centimeters
1 foot (ft)	34 centimeters
1 yard	.914 meters
1 mile	1.609 kilometers

Area

1 square foot	929.03 square cm
1 square yard	0.836 square meters
1 acre	0.405 hectares
1 square mile	258.999 hectares

Weight

1 ounce	28.35 grams
1 pound	0.453 kilograms
	(454 grams)
1 ton	0.907 metric tons
(2,000 pounds)	(907.18) kilograms

Volume (liquid)

1 ounce	30 milliliters
1 cup	236 millileters
1 quart liquid	0.95 liter
1 gallon	3.78 liters

Metric to U.S.

Distance

1 centimeter	0.394 inch
1 meter	39.37 inches
	3.28 feet
1 kilometer	0.621 mile

Area

1 square meter	1.196 square yards
	10.764 square feet
1 hectare	2.471 acres
1 square kilometer	0.386 square miles

Weight

1 gram	0.035 ounces
1 kilogram	2.205 pounds
1 metric ton	1.102 tons
(1000 kilograms)	

Liquid

1 liter	1.057 liquid quarts
	33.82 ounces
1 milliliter	0.034 ounces

See directions on page 28.

REPORT

Topic _____

Title of book: _____

Author: _____

Illustrator: _____

Publisher: _____

Copyright date: _____   Number of pages: _____

    Tell what you learned from this book, or, draw a picture of something you learned from this book.

_____

_____

_____

_____

_____

_____

_____

See directions on page 28.

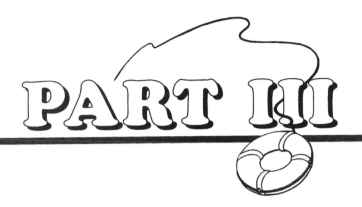

PART III

Answers

Answers

In the Lunchroom - 2, Page R3

Match.

1. G
2. C
3. A
4. F
5. B
6. E
7. H
8. D

In the Lunchroom - 3, Page R4

Listen, read, and write.

standing
lunch
carrying
brought
opening
sandwich
juice
laughing
homework
throwing
garbage

In the Library - 2, Page R9

YES or NO?

1. no
2. no
3. yes
4. no
5. no
6. no
7. no
8. yes

In the Library - 3, Page R10

Listen, read, and write.

librarian
helping
checking out
returning
magazine
headphones
dictionary
taking
shelf
encyclopedia

In the Library - 5, Page R12

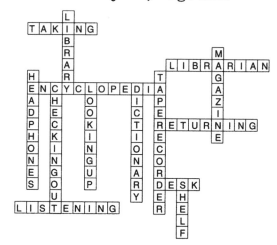

In the Nurse's Office - 5, Page R17

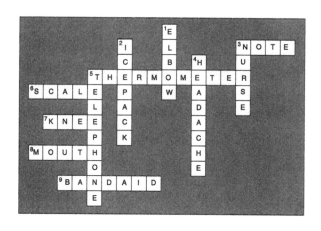

In the Nurse's Office - 2, Page R14

YES or NO?

1. no
2. no
3. yes
4. no
5. yes
6. no
7. no

In the Nurse's Office - 3, Page R15

Listen, read , and write.

nurse
scale
waiting
sick
headache
thermometer
hurt
ice pack
band aid
bringing

In Science Class - 2, Page R19

Match.

1. G
2. F
3. A
4. B
5. C
6. I
7. H
8. E
9. D

In Science Class - 3, Page R20

Listen, read , and write.

studying
observing
mice
feeding
cage
whales
turtle
terrarium
labeling
penguins
report
dolphins
iguana

In Science Class - 5, Page R22

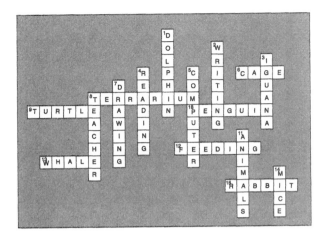

In the Computer Room - 2, Page R24

YES or NO?

1. no
2. no
3. yes
4. yes
5. no
6. yes
7. yes
8. no
9. yes

In the Computer Room - 3, Page R25

Listen, read, and write.

room
banner
floppy disk
disk drive
keyboard
printing
teaching
mouse
screen
work

In the Computer Room - 4, Page R26

1. keyboard
2. CD
3. cursor
4. on/off button
5. screen
6. monitor

In the Computer Room - 5, Page R27

The Grasshopper and the Ant - 2, Page R29

Listen, read, and write.

loved
work
summer
plenty
winter
easy
saving
laughed
nothing
remembered
grasshopper
closed

The Grasshopper and the Ants - 3, Page R30

Match the opposites

1. F
2. G
3. E
4. D
5. C
6. B
7. A

Fill in the correct squares:

1. the grasshopper
2. the ants
3. the grasshopper
4. the ants
5. the grasshopper
6. the ants
7. the ants

The Grasshopper and the Ants - 4, Page R31

```
G Q G U E K E W Y J C B B Y
L M L Y W A A G T E O T T U
I D S O O N S Y S P L A Y I
K Q W A R M Y Y E H D S B Q
E D J L K M S M X O Q M E G
G R A S S H O P P E R M Y I
A E D U T H A N T E O T Z V
R E M E M B E R K C N E D E
E C L O S E D N B E X H N N
H L S U M M E R L D U U O R
F O O D I W H P M A T N X S
N N H H Y W I N T E R G M O
Q G L A U G H E D B U R D M
F C D E U V E A W A Y Y T E
```

The Hungry Fox - 2, Page R34

Listen, read and write.

shepherd
hole
place
dinner
hungry
what

Finally
squeezed
much
fat
nobody
stuck

The Hungry Fox - 3, Page R35

Match verb forms

1. F
2. C
3. E
4. D
5. A
6. B

YES or NO?

1. no
2. no
3. no
4. yes
5. yes
6. yes
7. yes
8. no

The Hungry Fox - 4, Page R36

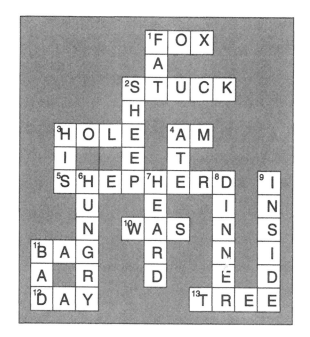

The Boy and the Wolf - 2, Page R39

Listen, read and write.

watching

boring

thought

people

Where

fooled

again

hungry

started

want

Nobody

The Boy and the Wolf - 3, Page R40

I. Put the sentences in the correct order.

2 a

8 b

4 c

1 d

6 e

7 f

5 g

3 h

Yes or No?

1. no
2. yes
3. no
4. yes
5. no
6. no
7. no.

The Boy and the Wolf - 4, Page R41

The Fox and the Wild Boar - 2, Page R44

Listen, read , and write.

woods

noise

terrible

rubbing

tusks

sharpening

safe

silly

danger

began

The Fox and the Wild Boar - 3, Page R45

Fill in the Correct Squares:
1. noisy
2. was rubbing his tusks
3. wanted sharp tusks
4. "You are safe here."
5. "Silly old fox."

The Fox and the Wild Boar - 4, Page R46

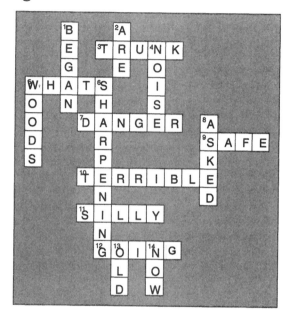

Scrambled Sentences - 1, Page R48
1. A boy was watching sheep.
2. The wolf ate all the sheep.
3. The people went back to work.
4. This job is boring.
5. Later a hungry wolf came.
6. He started to eat the sheep.
7. Nobody came to help the boy.

Scrambled Sentences - 2, Page R49
1. What's that terrible noise?
2. I must make my tasks sharp now.
3. He began to rub his tusks again.
4. What a good dinner that is!
5. He was stuck inside the tree.
6. A hungry fox was watching a shepherd.

7. This is a good place to hide my dinner.
8. The grasshopper did not like to work.

Zoo or Farm?, Page R50
Zoo: seals, alligator, panda, koala bear, lion, kangaroo

Farm: sheep, horse, cow, duck, goat, pig

What Animals Belong Together?, Page R51
Row 1. cow, horse, pig, sheep.
Row 2. grasshopper, spider, bee, beetle
Row 3. octopus, seahorse, shark, fish
Row 4. elephant, zebra, giraffe, kangaroo

How Do Animals Move?, Page R52
Fly: bee, bat, owl
Hop/Jump: grasshopper, frog, rabbit
Walk/run: zebra, bear, moose
Swim: seal, dolphin, whale

Fur, Feathers or Scales?, Page R53
Fur: panda, deer, fox, camel
Feathers: hawk, ostrich, turkey, flamingo
Scales: crocodile, lizard, fish, iguana

Animals and Their Babies, Page R54
1. C
2. G
3. D
4. B
5. H
6. A
7. E
8. F

What Do Animals Eat? Page R54

Plants: deer, zebra, elephant, rabbit, hippopotamus, giraffe.

Animals: seal, polar bear, owl, tiger, crocodile, eagle.

What's the Temperature? - 1, Page R56

1. twenty degrees Fahrenheit
2. eighty degrees Fahrenheit
3. fifteen degrees Fahrenheit

What's the Temperature?-3, Page R58

1. thermometers
2. temperature
3. Fahrenheit and Celsius
4. 60°
5. 32°
6. 212°
7. 98.6°
8. fever
9. Answers vary
10. Answers vary

What's the Temperature? - 4, Page R59

1. 90°
2. 10°
3. 70°
4. 50°
5. 98.6°
6. 103°
1. ??
2. ??
3. ??

The Parts of a Plant-2, Page R69

1. roots
2. flowers, flowering plants
3. soil, minerals
4. stem, leaves
5. photosynthesis
6. Seeds, plants

Parts of a Plant - 3, Page R70

YES or NO?

1. no
2. no
3. no
4. yes
5. yes
6. no
7. yes
8. yes

Match.

1. F
2. D
3. A
4. C
5. B
6. E

How Flowers Make Seeds - 2, Page R72

1. stamen, pistil
2. pollen, falls, fertilization
3. ovary, seeds
4. fruits, vegetables, hold

How Flowers Make Seeds - 3, Page R73

I. YES or NO?

1. yes
2. no
3. no
4. yes

II. Match.

1. B
2. F
3. A
4. E
5. C
6. *D*

III. apple, tomato, cherry, orange, peas, green beans, strawberry

Plant Quiz, Page R74

1. E
2. C
3. H
4. J
5. I
6. K
7. A
8. B
9. L
10. F
11. G
12. D

Label the Parts of the Plant, Page R75

1. stamen
2. ovary
3. sepal
4. receptacle
5. fruit
6. seed
7. pistil
8. pollen
9. petal
10. flower
11. leaf
12. stem
13. roots

Write the numbers, Page R76

a. 7, 4, 5, 2
b. 10, 9, 3, 8
c. 0, 6, 11, 13
d. 15, 18, 20, 12
e. 30, 14, 40, 50
f. 25, 37, 48
g. 87, 93, 52
h. 100, 210
i. 412, 913
j. 824

k. 359
l. 1,000, 4,700
m. 5,824
n. 8,493
o. 2,629

Draw the hands on the clocks, Page R77

What time is it? R78

A. It's eight o'clock.
B. It's eight ten.
    It's ten minutes after (past) eight.
C. It's eight fifteen.
    It's fifteen minutes after (past) eight.
    It's a quarter after (past) eight.
D. It's eight twenty-five.
    It's twenty-five after (past) eight.
E. It's eight thirty.
    It's half past eight.
F. It's eight thirty-five.
    It's twenty-five minutes to nine.
G. It's eight forty-five.
    It's fifteen minutes to nine.
    It's a quarter to nine.
H. It's eight fifty-nine.
    It's one minute to nine.
I. It's nine o'clock.

Math Symbols, Page R79

2. 6 - 2 = 4
3. 5 x 10=50
4. 12 ÷ 4 = 3
5. 8 > 7
6. 9 < 11
7. 25¢
8. $6.00
9. 100%
10. $5^2 = 25$
11. $\sqrt{9} = 3$

Read and Write with Math Symbols, Page R 80

1b. Eight minus three equals five.
 c. Four times six equals twenty-four.
2a. Ten minus two equals five.
 b. Twelve divided by three equals four.
 c. Eight is greater than seven.
3a. Three is less than four.
 b. ten percent
 c. twenty cents
4a. three dollars and forty-five cents
 b. the square root of sixteen
 c. three square

The Multiplication Tables, Page R81

1. zero
2. five
3 eight
4. three
5. twelve
6. five
7. Answers will vary.

How Much Is It?, Page R83

a. 25¢
b. 10¢
c. 5¢
d. 1¢

e. 35¢
f. 11¢
g. 40¢
h. 3¢
i. 15¢
j. 16¢
k. 50¢
l. 26¢
m. 25¢
n. 36¢
o. 27¢
p. 41¢

Read and Write About Money, Page R84

d. seventy-five cents
e. one dollar and seventy-five cents
 a dollar seventy-five
f. twenty-eight dollars and eighty-five cents
 twenty-eight eighty-five
g. sixty-seven dollars and one cent
 sixty-seven oh one
h. forty four dollars and twenty-nine cents
 forty-four twenty-nine

Solve Word Problems - 1, Page R85

a. ten dollars
b. eleven books
c. one hundred sixty
d. eight dollars

Solve Word Problems - 2, Page R86

a. five dollars
b. six dollars
c. five cookies
d. five gifts

Solve Word Problems - 3, Page R87

   a. sixty cents (60¢)

   b. twelve dollars ($12.00)

   c. thirty miles

   d. eight boxes

Solve Word Problems - 4, Page R88

   a. ten cents (10¢)

   b. four students

   c. four students

   d. six

Reading Numbers: Ordinals, Page R89

   1. Miguel

   2. Shantra

   3. Joe

   4. Miss Rose

   5. Akiko

Place Values - 1, Page R90

   d. ones

   e. tens

   f. hundreds

   g. thousands

   h. thousands

   i. 1,058

Place Values - 2, Page R91

   b. thousands

   c. ten thousands

   d. hundred thousands

   g. three hundred ninety-seven thousand, five hundred one.

   h. four hundred seven thousand, eight hundred sixty-nine.

Read and Write Large Numbers, Page R93

   a. 1,285   b. 48,035   c. 68,904

   d. 431,800   e. 10,973,000

   f. 2,420,021,527   g. 9,674,310,530

   a. one thousand two hundred eighty-five

   b. forty-eight thousand thirty-five

   c. sixty-eight thousand nine hundred four

   d. four hundred thirty-one thousand eight hundred

   e. ten million nine hundred seventy-three thousand

   f. two billion four hundred twenty million, twenty one thousand, five hundred twenty-seven

   g. nine billion, six hundred seventy-four million, three hundred ten thousand, five hundred thirty

Different Ways of Reading Numbers, Page R94

   a. Three hundred and forty-two

   b. Three forty two

   c. One thousand three hundred forty-two

   d. Thirteen hundred forty-two

   e. October 10, thirteen forty-two

   f. (six oh nine) five five one three four two

Math Terms, Page R95

   3. 2, 4, 6, 8, 10, 12, 14, 16, 18

   4. $5 \times 2 = 10$

   5a. 617

   b. 315

   6a. 1,022

   b. 200

   7a. 2,930, 14,490

   b. 2,900   14,500

   c. 3,000   14,000

Different Kinds of Numbers, Page R96

   1. G
   2. E
   3. A
   4. B
   5. F
   6. I
   7. D
   8. C
   9. H

Fractions, Page R97

   i. $\frac{3}{4}$; three fourths

   j. $\frac{2}{5}$; two fifths

   k. $\frac{3}{8}$; three eighths

   l. $\frac{5}{8}$; five eighths

   m. $1\frac{1}{2}$; one and one half

   n. $2\frac{3}{4}$; two and three fourths

   o. $\frac{5}{6}$

   p. $1\frac{1}{3}$

Fractions-2, Page R98

   c. $\frac{2}{5}$, $\frac{3}{5}$

   d. $\frac{3}{4}$, $\frac{1}{4}$; $\frac{5}{6}$, $\frac{1}{6}$; $\frac{5}{8}$, $\frac{3}{8}$

Decimal Numbers, Page R99

   h. 1. .3
      2. 1.4
      3. .05
      4. 2.15

Angles and Triangles, R101

   1. D
   2. G
   3. H
   4. F
   5. A
   6. E
   7. C
   8. B

Circles, Page R103

   a. radius
   c. circumference
   d. 9.42

How long is this pencil?, Page R105

   A. 5
   B. 6 inches long.
   C. is 4 inches long.
   D. The eraser is 2 inches long.
   E. The marker is 3 inches long.

How tall are these people?, Page R106

   2. four
   3. six feet tall.
   5. four feet, six inches tall.
   6. is five feet tall.
   7. is six feet, six inches tall.

Long, Wide and High, Page R107

   1. four, one, two
   2. eleven, eight and a half

Change Feet to Inches, Page R109

   1. 2
   2. 3
   3. 4
   4. 1
   5. 60

6. 24
7. 15
8. 28
9. 38
10. 49

Measuring Liquids - 2, Page R111

a. pint
b. quart
c. cups
d. quarts
e. 16
f. 8
g. 4
h. 2
i. 8, 4, gallon

Measuring Liquids- 3, Page R112

1. gallon
2. pint
3. quart
4. tablespoon
5. ounce
6. two
7. eight
8. sixteen
9. thirty-two
10. four
11. four
12. four
13. eight

How much do these things weigh?, Page R113

1. book
2. boy
3. elephant

Where Is the United States? Page R116

1. continent
2. country
3. east, Pacific
4. Canada
5. south
6. neighbors

The Fifty States, Page R118

1. fifty
2. Hawaii, Alaska
3. islands
4. Canada
5. Alaska
6. United States
7. Washington, D.C.

The Map of the United States, Page R120

1. fifty
4. California, Oregon, Washington
5. Maine, Massachusetts, New Hampshire, Connecticut, Rhode Island, New York, New Jersey, Delaware, Maryland, Virginia, North Carolina, South Carolina, Georgia, Florida
6. Maine, New Hampshire, Vermont, New York, Michigan, Minnesota, Wisconsin, North Dakota, Montana, Idaho, Washington. (Ohio and Pennsylvania touch Lake Erie, which touches Canada.)

Page R121

7. Texas, New Mexico, Arizona, California
8. Florida, Alabama, Mississippi, Louisiana, Texas
9. Nevada, Utah, Colorado, Kansas
10. New Jersey, Pennsylvania, Ohio, Indiana, Illinois, Iowa, (Missouri), Nebraska, Wyoming, Utah, Nevada, California

11. North Dakota, South Dakota, Nebraska, Kansas, Oklahoma, Texas.

12. Louisiana, Arkansas, Missouri, Iowa, Minnesota

Page R122

13. New Hampshire, New Jersey, New Mexico, New York

14. North Dakota, South Dakota, North Carolina, South Carolina, West Virginia

United States Word Search, Page R124

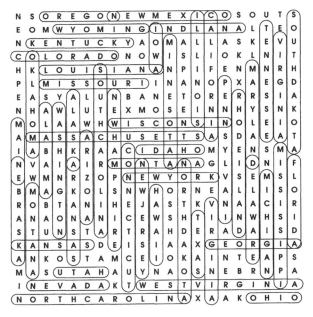

The United States: Land and Water - 2, Page R126

1. Rocky
2. Appalachian
3. river
4. five
5. Idaho, Montana, Colorado, Wyoming, Nevada, Utah, Arizona, New Mexico
6. New York, Pennsylvania, Ohio, Michigan, Indiana, Illinois, Wisconsin, Minnesota

Facts About the United States: Quiz, Page R127

Match

1. D
2. A
3. B
4. C
5. G
6. F
7. E
8. J
9. I
10. K
11. L
12. H

The People of the United States, Page R129

1. c
2. d
3. immigrants, immigrants
4. b
5. a

The Leaders of the United States, Page R131

1. (Current president's name)
2. (Current vice president's name)
3. in the White House, in Washington, D.C.
4. Every four years, in November
5. the people
6. the Congress; the Senators and Representatives

Symbols of the United States, Page R133

1. New York Harbor
2. Red, white and blue
3. 50, 13
4. a symbol of the government of the United States

5. bald eagle
6. The Star-Spangled Banner
7. Independence Hall, Philadelphia, Pennsylvania

My State, Page R134

Answers depend on state.

My Town, Page R134

Answers depend on local community.

The First People In America, Page R138

1. no
2. twenty thousand
3. Asia
4. North and South
5. cities
6. villages
7. animals
8. Native Americans

Columbus Comes to America, Page R140

1. 1492
2. China and the Indies (or Japan)
3. Indians
4. four
5. Spain

Colonies in North America, Page R142

1. kings and queens
2. Mexico, Florida, Central and South America
3. Canada, Louisiana
4. North America
5. East Coast

Why Did People Come to America?, Page R144

1. gold
2. Native Americans
3. Christianity
4. religious
5. servants
6. slaves

The Thirteen English Colonies, Page R146

1. C
2. A
3. D
4. B
5. New Hampshire, Massachusetts, Connecticut, Rhode Island, New York, Pennsylvania, New Jersey, Delaware, Maryland, Virginia, North Carolina, South Carolina, Georgia

Americans Have Trouble with England, Page R148

1. France
2. England
3. Canada
4. pay
5. taxes
6. not
7. colonies, angry
8. 1775

The Birth of the United States, Page R150

1. Philadelphia
2. independence
3. King George
4. Thomas Jefferson
5. Independence
6. 1776, the United States
7. George Washington

The New Government of the United States, Page 152

1. king
2. people
3. Constitution
4. George Washington
5. father
6. Jefferson

Early American History: Quiz, Page R153

1. C
2. H
3. I
4. K
5. D
6. F
7. A
8. J
9. E
10. G
11. B

Crossword Puzzle, Page R154

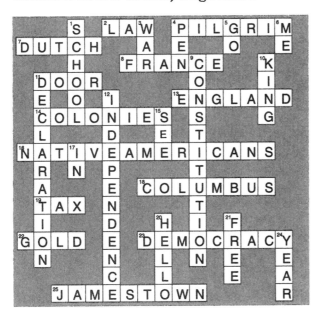

The Three Branches of Government - 2, Page R157

1. three
2. laws
3. legislative
4. Senate, representatives
5. two
6. six
7. representatives
8. (current state senators)
9. two
10. (current district representative)

The Three Branches of Government - 4, Page R159

1. executive
2. enforces
3. many
4. cabinet
5. interpret
6. judicial
7. Supreme
8. appoints

The Three Branches of Government - 5, Page R160

I. *List*.

Legislative: Congress, Senators, make laws, representatives

Executive: president, vice president, enforce laws, cabinet

Judicial: Supreme Court, interpret laws, decide if someone has broken a law, judge

II. *Match*.

1. B
2. C
3. A
4. D